On Dive Bars:

"I don't enjoy dive bars," said no decent person ever.

If you don't love a good dive bar, you have no soul. You are a shallow and hopelessly tasteless blob of tissue who has falsely convinced yourself that you're better than cheap beer, stale bar snacks, and fart jokes.

On *The Watering Hole:*

The watering hole is where all of the drama occurs. It's where lions hydrate alongside antelope, and where former jailbirds clink glasses with officers of the law. It's where a hippopotamus enjoys a bath with their young playing in close proximity to ancient and predatory monster reptiles, and where protective fathers hesitantly drop-off their newly-legal daughters for their very first ladies' night out. It's where birds play musical chairs on the backs of elephants and giraffe, and where two sexually-bored married couples mingle with each other and negotiate a swinger's night amongst themselves.

I feel that the watering hole is important. It's friends, it's family, it's love, it's sadness, it's funny, it's loud, it's home. It's a sanctuary of celebration as well as mourning. It's a place to meet and discuss business as well as get tanked and watch the big game. It's a place where relationships begin and end. It's a place where local musicians can showcase their talent, and where the town drunkard can re-live his garage band days with some karaoke. It's a place where advice is given and taken, and where people who would otherwise be strangers build bonds that can last a lifetime. It's a place of storytelling; where the old man at the end of the bar shares tales with future old men at the end of the bar. It's a place of poor health habits, yet at the same time, it can prove to be the healthiest of venues to step foot into. It's dirty. It's stinky. It's overpriced. It's loud. It's pure magic, and it's a place worthy of a book...

For my family...

and for Joe Rogan—I had to. It was a bet.

Topics Explored:

Acknowledgements

Crikey—where do I begin? I guess I'll start with those of whom I've served in the trenches with; bartenders like Danny, Art, Laff, Pete, Greeny, Casey, Teen, and Kat—I learned everything from you guys. I'd also like to pay my sincere homage to my loyal band of regulars and other co-workers: Lou and Rose; Wild Bill and Mary; Joey and Matty; Bob and Marg; Traci; Keith; Ant and Tara; the Campbells; Kera and Albert; Kelly, Kelly, Lea, and Rach; Bob and Karen; Kevin Looney; Rusty and Kate; Fran and Tom; Jay and Tiff; Courtney, Amanda, Josh, Erin, and the rest of your insane crew; Meg; Tony Kenny and your amigos; the Sicilian; Chuck; Alex "Tina" Converse; Mary Beach; and to those of you whose names I can't recall. Yeah, yeah—you too, Glen. It was the greatest honor of my life to pour beers for you all week-in and week-out, and to simply be in your company so often. I miss you all dearly.

Next, I'd like to thank those on the logistical side of the writing process. Muchas gracias, besos, y abrazos muy fuertes a mis profesores en TCNJ, especialmente Dra. Morin, Dr. Figueroa, and Dra. Compte, for all of your counseling through the years. Many thanks to Kate and Nick for giving me the vitamins needed to maintain my strength, and to Brad and D'Anne for the film and photo side of it all. And a sincere thanks to you, Jessica, for helping me during all of those late-night grammar emergencies.

Thank you Conor (my barback) for bailing me out of countless nights spent lost in the weeds.

It's important for me to thank my friends—both old and new—who didn't necessarily have much to do with this book, but whose support willed me through this process and inspired me to keep going after this one. Big hugs, kisses, and ass-cheek slaps (to Todd, especially) to my friends at the Farm and Fisherman Tavern; the Gellermans and Puja; Matt, Daniela, and to your extended families; Cliff, Jennifer, and to your extended families as well; Iggy and Rach; Ian Hall; Sandy; Nick Pasqua; Krysti—for not having murdered me yet; and PJ— I can't thank you enough for all that you've done for me over the years. The farm will always be in my heart.

Thank you to my family: the Reids, the Holbrooks, and our clan across the pond in Glasgow. More specifically, thanks to Mom, Dad, Kasey, and my hairy collaborator Simba for all of the help and support—for as far back as I can remember it. You guys are everything to me. Thanks to Nana for always keeping my belly full, and for being the best Friday night date a guy could ask for. Thanks to Uncle G.A., Aunt Denise, Uncle Jeff, Aunt Heather, Marc, Chris, Jefferey, Brittany, and Cammy—I love you all. I also want to publicly thank Kathleen. You are the strongest beacon of inspiration in my life, and your refusal for mediocrity urges me to be better.

Lastly, to the reader: although big publishers may not have given me a chance yet, it appears that you have. That means more to me than anything.

The Watering Hole

A Bartender's Breakdown
of the Bipedal Drinking Establishment

Jay Reid

Author's Note:

I have changed the names of several of the characters in the book as to protect their superhero identities.

For more information on this book or any other of Jay Reid's works, please visit www.jayreidwrites.com

DISCLAIMER

If you dwell in a world of political correctness, put this thing down and move onto the self-help section. This is a book about bars and barroom behavior: dirty, disgusting, hilarious, obnoxious, inappropriate behavior.

In the chapters to come, I talk about sex, drugs, and drunkenness. I curse like a sailor, and I even graphically describe what I imagine a particular undesirable bar regular's vagina looks like—amongst other questionably offensive tales of pillage and plunder, of course. Oh, and if you're a serial one-star restaurant reviewer on *Yelp*, the odds of you liking this book are not very good, and I probably don't like you, either.

This is not a memoir. Yes, throughout the following pages I do include a number of personal anecdotes as well as those of other bartenders and bar guests. I do so, however, in order to assist in the illustration of the main ideas and talking points of this book.

There are many books that have been written by bartenders that offer lengthy and detailed autobiographies, with many of them proving to be very entertaining reads. Chef and television host Anthony Bourdain wrote a unique book titled *Kitchen Confidential* that not only served as a memoir but a philosophical platform as he dissected the culture and lifestyle of one who calls the back of the house their home. But that's not what this book is. This is a collaborative analysis of one of the most amazing and fucked-up places known to man: the local drinking establishment.

I'd also like to point out that as much of a fan as I am of the fields of psychology and anthropology, I have no degree or formal education in either. This book contains a *lot* of discussion of the two, so if I offend anyone who may teach this stuff in front of a class or write scholarly journals about these topics, I offer you my deepest fake and sarcastic apology.

Relax people. Save your hate mail and insulting Twitter messages for the next guy who claims to know everything. My dad's already beat you to it by reminding me on many, many occasions that I'm not the brightest tool in the chandelier.

This book should be seen as a lighthearted breakdown of a place and community that many of us visit on a weekly or daily basis; an essential and vital point in longitude and latitude in many of our lives; an environment that's essence tends to fly under the radar of popular recognition and proper acknowledgment.

On Sounding Like A Miserable Turd

I'm not going to bullshit you—there *is* a fair amount of griping, complaining, and over-exaggerating in this book. It's important to take into account, however, that it's all in good fun. As angry and negative as I may seem at times, I truly love being behind the bar—most bartenders do—and I'm fascinated beyond my public school vocabulary with this topic and all of the strangeness that surrounds it.

On The Setting

This satirical case study focuses primarily on the bars in which I have worked. I would have loved, in fact, to travel the country and beyond to conduct in-depth interviews with living legend barkeeps that man the helm of some of the most famous and notorious drinking establishments in the world. But for the sake of this particular project, I felt it best to keep it as intimate as possible. I focused my binoculars at a smaller and more concise sample of watering holes and their inhabitants.

How To Read This Book

Pretend that you are with your friends spread out on some couches with your favorite beer in hand, all of you tuned into a specialized nature documentary that seeks to analyze the bars that you like to frequent the most. After reading this book, I hope that you not only become more conscious and appreciative of the watering hole that you like to visit, but also that you'll laugh and cry at some of the stuff I've written down...and that you'll tip your bartender.

How This All Started

As I was sitting in a cafe pondering the beginning of this book and how I should introduce it, I was left with a bitter taste in my mouth about the whole thing. In that moment, I *hated* bartending. I hated everything about it —especially the idea of this book that I had already spent more than two years working on. I was ready to quit my job and hit the delete button, casting my manuscript into the abyss.

Why all the whiny melodrama? Well, I recently had one of those shifts behind the bar that are inevitable for all bartenders. Every guest seemed to be in cahoots with one another on a mission to rob me of my will and sanity. I even entertained the possibility of these people chatting on the message board at *Weareallassholes.com* and holding their monthly meeting at my bar that evening. Besides having to play the role of a disciplinarian with an individual twice my age, I had to apologize to several guests for their undercooked and unacceptable entrees as they condescendingly reprimanded me (as if I had actually cooked their food) and angrily demanded refunds.

The barrage was endless: complaints, obnoxious behavior, and strange happenings galore. And to top my night off, a girl threw her credit card at me as if it was a serrated ninja star and wrote a big, bold *$0* on the tip line of her receipt, with the kind words "you suck" on the back. Why did she do this? Clearly because she was curator of the meeting. I chased her out of the building cursing her to the high heavens, warning her to never step her bitchy feet back onto the property. I had all I could take. "Last call," I yelled at about 10pm. "I hate this fucking job."

So I sat there in that cafe contemplating whether or not to scrap this whole book. Why would I want to write about something that I have begun to hate? Why work so hard on examining this stuff when it was now nothing more of a source of irritation to me?

I willfully focused on the good. Sounds like something Mr. Miyagi would say, I know. But choosing what to focus on is a precious life skill. Losing focus is such an easy thing to do the second you have to put up with someone's drunken nonsense, but I try to remind myself time and time again that I'm surrounded by people who, for the most part, like me. I focused on them.

They come from all walks of life to enjoy a beer and some bar food, but most of all, they come for my company. I love this job because I rub elbows with such an eclectic and strange variety of people all at once. I get paid to socialize. I fill my pockets with cash and girls' phone numbers. I am told intimate, precious things by friends and strangers alike that may go unheard by those closest to them. I am trusted. I'm in a great position to network and receive police affiliation cards to get me out of tickets. I see cleavage everywhere. I am the temporary host of this grandiose party that goes until 2 am. It's honoring, humbling, and can often be really weird.

So, with all of that in mind, I continued with the book because I feel that the watering hole is important. It's friends, it's family, it's love, it's sadness, it's funny, it's loud, it's home. It's a sanctuary of celebration as well as mourning. It's a place to meet and discuss business as well as get tanked and watch the big game. It's a place where relationships begin and end. It's a place where local musicians can showcase their talent, and where the town drunkard can re-live his garage band days with some karaoke. It's a place where advice is given and taken, and where people who would otherwise be strangers build bonds that can last a lifetime. It's a place of storytelling, where the old man at the end of the bar recounts, for the 600th time, the story of the big fish he caught that somehow grew 10 feet in length over the years, all while an audience of future old men at the end of the bar cling to his every word. It's a place of poor health habits, yet at the same time, it can prove to be the healthiest of places to step foot into. It's dirty. It's stinky. It's overpriced. It's loud. It's pure magic. It's a place worthy of a book, and that is the mindset that has seen me through this process.

Willy

Since this is a play on nature documentaries, this book wouldn't be complete without an overly-animated and enthusiastic nature expert doing all of the grunt work. I needed to find the quintessential, stereotypical, bushwhacked Australian with dirty safari attire, pit stains, and an accent thicker than crocodile skin. For that, Willy has been sent out of my imagination and into the trenches of some local pubs to conduct reconnaissance of the natives. His italicized notes will introduce each topic before it's discussed further. He's a little rough around the edges, and his people skills have diminished a bit over years and years spent alone on various observation assignments in the bush, but he's a good guy. I hope you enjoy his work.

Now, I'd like to formally welcome you to *The Watering Hole*! Proceed with caution and a minimal amount of sobriety. Keeping a plastic bag and some hand sanitizer handy is a good idea as well, as it's about to get messy!

1
Insertion

I met Jay a few years back at a bar in San Diego, as I was in town for a day or two before heading south to Guadalupe Island to swim with Great White Sharks. He struck me as an odd fellow; a curious chap who seemed overly-interested in my stories. But hey—he sure-as-hell could pour a mean drink.

He tracked me down recently and asked me to help him with a book he wanted to write about the ecosystem of the bipedal drinking establishment. Honestly, I think he actually got the idea from me, but as I had been gored in the ass by a rhino several weeks earlier, I figured that I could use a bit of a break from the dangers of the wild. I agreed to help him, but I had no idea what I was getting myself into.

I've been a bushman for many years, and during that time, I've had lots of close calls. I've had to run from a stampeding herd of elephants, as well as take cover during an all-out war amongst two communities of angry, territorial chimps. I've been bitten by crocs, punched and kicked by kangaroos, spit at by cobras, shat on by birds, licked by llamas, and mounted and humped by several different primates who apparently found me attractive. All of the abuse I've taken and strange

1

events I've witnessed in the wild had me believe that I'd be well-suited to document the bipedal drinking hole.

Right from the get-go, however, I was aggressively stared-down by a group of men who resembled a pack of hungry wolves I once followed in British Columbia. I was poked, gawked, and laughed at by a woman who reminded me of an ostrich or emu I grew up with on my farm in Australia. My foot was stepped on by a gentleman who weighed more than a half-grown hippo I filmed in Africa. An old woman farted in my general direction which resulted in a stench beyond the power of any northeastern United States skunk. After I had a glimpse of an attractive female, I was punched in the eye by her alpha boyfriend who hit harder than the silverback I was once clubbed by in the Congo. I could deal with all of that, but when I was cornered, solicited, and howled at by a creature called a 'Deloris,' I hit the brink. She executed her mating call, grabbed me bum, and sank her claws in. For the first time in my life, I had to visit a shrink.

When Jay approached me and asked me if I wanted to help document this barroom environment and all of the creatures that frequent it, I thought 'how hard can it be?! I'll take some photos, write some notes, have a few drinks, and maybe bang a few broads.' Crikey, was I naive about the whole thing! There's a lot more to the human watering hole that meets the eye, and I did my best to capture the true essence of this insanely wild place.

***

The one question that I have asked myself the most while bartending, both under circumstances of extreme jubilance and gnawing stress, is *just how the hell did I end up behind the bar?*

Once upon a time, I had fairly normal job descriptions and school schedules. Up until the moment I had stepped behind the bar for the first time, I worked in construction, plumbing, and landscaping. I also punched the time card at a sporting goods store, a supermarket, and a neighborhood ice rink as a "skate guard." For that gig, several days a week I wore a reflective vest and carried a walkie-talkie as I sharked around the rink during public skating times tasked with enforcing the company's rules, and ensuring that everyone was behaving in a safe manner. What I was really concerned with doing, however, was practicing my own skating for playing ice hockey, and hitting on cute girls, of course.

I even did some time as a United States Navy sailor. It was while I swabbed the poop deck that I was introduced to the most beautiful city that I had ever set my eyes on: San Diego. After my time in the fleet, I decided to make myself a home in the whales vagina. But what I would do with all of that sunshine, perfect surf, and abundance of hot babes was yet to be determined.

My days spent beach-bumming it were great. There seemed to be waves every day (something almost unheard of for an east coast surfer like myself), and I had almost zero responsibility. As many servicemen who switch back to civilian life do, I collected unemployment as well as worked under-the-table for a plumber, so I had plenty of money saved to live on for a while. My path changed dramatically, however, when I stumbled upon an advertisement in the newspaper for classes at a nearby bartending school. I decided to give it a shot just for the hell of it.

The Academy

Other than helping you to memorize cocktails and to harness a proper pour count, bartending school is an utter waste of time and money. I spent two weeks associating the ingredients of classic cocktails like the *Godfather* (scotch and amaretto) with phrases like "shoots assholes"—mnemonic devices to help you remember what went with what. Everything that was touched upon was something that one could easily learn and practice at home—and for hundreds of dollars less.

But who doesn't love getting a certificate?! Upon completing the course, I was given a rinky-dink piece of paper with my name on it declaring that I was now a "certified bartender." In all reality, I was far from it. I wasn't even green enough to be called a young grasshopper. I was but a simple nymph.

The Job Hunt

Now that I was a hotshot graduate of the nearby bartending academy, I was ready to pop bottles and get paid! Well, *I* thought I was ready, but it just so happened that every single bar manager I handed my résumé to either laughed at my ambition, or simply bestowed upon me a look of pity—as if I was a vertically-challenged boy telling the high school basketball coach that I was going to turn pro one day.

Door to door I marched up and down the streets of downtown San Diego and its surrounding areas, handing out my information to managers who were polite enough to meet with me momentarily, but who all had said the same thing: "Try next door...I think they're hiring..."

It didn't take me long before I realized that I was stuck in the catch 22 of the hospitality industry: if you don't have experience, almost no one will hire you. But you can't *get* experience unless someone hires you. I scratched my head as I trudged out of yet another disappointing job interview trying to figure out where to go and what to do next.

Persistence eventually paid off and I was given a lead to a place that was to be casting interviews for a second wave of staff after opening only a few months prior. Now, I was reluctant to go because I figured that there would be a ton of applicants, and that I would get weeded-out as soon as they saw that I had zero bartending experience. But, to be honest, I was surfed-out for the time being, and my bank account was beginning to reach the danger zone. It was time to get me a jobby!

The building was stunning! It was located on Fifth Avenue only a few blocks from the convention center. I walked in with no expectations, and frankly, nowhere else to go. I sold myself well as I played the angle of a hardened north-easterner with a cutthroat work ethic. It worked. I got offered a job—as a barback. I took it.

Barbacking

I've been an athlete my whole life, but after my first shift as a barback on a busy Saturday night at this new and high-volume watering hole in downtown San Diego, I was out of breath.

I arrived at 3pm and was given my uniform, which basically consisted of a brown t-shirt. Then, without much instruction or guidance, I was told to "follow him." Basically, I was to shadow another barback that night, learn from him, and help him whenever I could. There were normally two barbacks on for a Saturday night, but there arose a problem shortly after we began to engage in small talk. The other guy who was supposed to be working that night called-out.

After a several minute crash-course in the geography of the monstrous bar/nightclub, I was on my own. I was more excited than anything, and after sizing myself up to my partner, my competitive side was quickly committed to outshining him. *I'm from New Jersey. I shovel snow—lots of it. What does this hippie know about hard work?*

A good barback is as hard to find as a little fruit fly swimming around in a Guinness, yet there is no more important tool in a busy bartender's arsenal. A barback is basically the bartender's bitch. He or she runs around like a junkie on speed, fetching supplies, restocking them, and cleaning up all of the bartender's messes while at the same time usually getting blamed for them. They roam about, shadowing their bartender just like remoras—those little fish that swim alongside of sharks. It's not a glamorous job by any means, but it's surely a necessary one at a high-volume drinking hole.

I spent the entire night weaving through hoards of horny, grinding bar guests as they dry-humped each other. I humped my *own* load—three 24-pack cases of bottled beer. I hustled to change kegs, burn the ice wells with scalding-hot water whenever one of the bartenders broke glass in one of them, and roamed the entire restaurant searching for glasses that were filled with cigarette butts, gum, napkins, and ripped-up drink coasters. I did all of this with the constant anxiety of making sure the bartenders had everything they needed to serve their guests.

A barback does all of the dirty work to allow for the bartender to do their job. They told me that the more time they had to spend fetching materials or cleaning up spills, the less time they had to promptly make drinks or bullshit with their customers, which in turn, would result in fewer tips for all of us. If the bartenders didn't do well, I certainly wasn't going to do well.

Being the runner isn't necessarily a job that requires a Ph.D. It does, however, require you to hustle your ass off, anticipate the needs of the bartenders, and to be patient and courteous to guests while doing so. As a barback, I wished many times that I had the remote control that Adam Sandler's character from the movie *Click* had and could pause time, put down the 3 cases of beer that I was trying to carry through a crowd of people that refused to move, and slap the shit out of everyone for being so unaccommodating.

I'm often asked by those young and old "How do I become a bartender?" I've gotten that question from pimply-faced college kids looking to make some extra cash, as well as middle-aged CPAs trying to meet new people shortly after a bitter divorce. Despite the lack of glamour, barbacking is probably the best path to pouring drinks in the big-time. It's hard work and probably won't get you laid, but it will allow you to get comfortable behind the bar while getting an insider's look at the tricks of the trade. Plus, the money isn't bad either. Many barbacks are paid a decent hourly wage plus 10% of the bartender's loot for the evening.

The Big Time

Before I knew it, I was clocking-in as a bartender and counting my own cash drawer. I got called-up to the big leagues from my position as a barback due to thinning of the herd. The chick who I was replacing cursed-out a guest the day prior and got fired, so I was asked to fill in. Although I had been working at this joint as a barback for several months now, there was still so much to learn. I was so afraid to make a mistake in fear that I might be exiled too.

At that time, I had already established my dominance as the top barback. I had the better shifts out of the other guys, and I was even paid a bit more in secret by the bartenders who acknowledged my hard work and efficiency. If I didn't perform as a bartender, I wasn't exactly confident that they'd just say "Oh well...you tried. Why don't you go back to being a barback?" That's not typically how things happen in restaurants. Once you go up, there's rarely any coming back down.

The night flew by and it was last call before I knew it. I managed to complete my first shift without any major errors. Yeah, there were a few specialty cocktails that I needed consultation on, and I think I switched-up someone's pomegranate martini with a french martini, but no one said anything. My first night was a rush, but I was glad it was over.

As our security crew was trying to guide all of the drunks out towards the street, a very attractive woman with bright red hair, a full-sleeve tattoo on her arm, and legs for days, turned and walked back towards the bar. I'd seen her there before and in other bars nearby, but she had never said hi to me. She made eye contact, smiled, and slowly closed the distance.

"Hey bartender!"

"What can I do for you, customer?" I learned that sassy reply from one of my co-workers.

Boobs—big, luscious, all-natural boobs had been delivered to me from the heavens as she pulled her shirt down and flashed me. My jaw dropped onto the bar top.

"I heard it was your first night...welcome to the club," she said in a raspy voice as she giggled, winked, and turned away. *Aha! She was a bartender as well!* It all made sense now.

"Oops. Almost forgot," she admitted as she placed a twenty-dollar bill right in front of me before blowing me a kiss goodnight. It was something I'd never forget, but something that wouldn't necessarily be a rarity in years to come.

Gaining My Sea Legs

I've logged over seven years behind the stick. I'm not a seasoned vet, but not necessarily green either. Since the aforementioned revealing of cleavage that I enjoyed my very first night behind the bar in downtown San Diego, I've worked in three different establishments before eventually moving back to California.

I slung drinks at an upscale Italian joint for a few years, an incredibly fun yet ever-changing Irish pub, and most recently, a family-oriented farm-to-table restaurant in Cherry Hill, New Jersey. I was a part of the opening staff for all three.

During the past several years, I went from being shy and timid, to being confident, outgoing, and even an obnoxious asshole on occasion. I learned more efficient ways of disarming aggressive drunks, as well as what liquors go well with what. I picked-up on the intricacies of meeting women and how to dance the line of customer versus hook-up. With the help of my fellow bartenders and servers, I stopped being so self-conscious and afraid to make mistakes, and instead, learned how to relax a bit and have fun.

Most of this book was written during my tenure at the Italian and Irish places, being that, during the writing period of this thing, those were the venues at which I was working. There's plenty of content from before and after the fact, but most of the tales told and thoughts put fourth in the following pages reflect the bulk of my memorable and influential experiences while tending bar at those spots.

2

The Gig

Those who call themselves 'bartenders' were the ones I was interested in documenting at first. I quickly learned that they are the zookeepers or bushmasters (in one form or another, hah!...get it?...zing!) of this environment. In other words, they run the show. They also spend, on average, more time at these human dwellings of drinking and dancing than most, and so I knew that they would have the inside story on many of the creatures that I would eventually encounter.

Bartending is a strange way to make a living—and that comes from a guy who spends the workday crawling around the bush at night talking to himself on a voice recorder. There was something off about each bartender I encountered—something strange about them that I couldn't exactly identify. Granted, I'm not necessarily an expert on people, but the bartenders in this study all proved to be very intriguing.

***

Never in a million years would I have guessed that I'd be conducting official business in a t-shirt and jeans, covered in spilled booze, and surrounded by such awesome people. The detour I took years ago that would eventually have me slinging drinks behind the bar in my late 20s was one that the career counselor at my high school failed to mention.

This was all by accident. I wanted to be a lot of things when I was growing up (and still do), but none of those things included being in the hospitality industry. Interestingly enough, if you talk to most bartenders about how they ended up pouring beers for a living, they'll probably admit the same thing. We all had dreams, and most of us still cling to them. But what I like to argue is that we're living it—*the dream*—every time we step behind the bar.

Bartending's Past

For as long as human beings have been escaping their living or working quarters in search of a mind-numbing break from it all, there have been those who have been there to assist them in doing so. It's known that during the turbulent reign of Julius Caesar, there were inns and salons at which men gathered to discuss politics, business, and probably even conspire to murder Julius Caesar. They did all of this, of course, over a drink or two. And like most people, they liked their beverages served to them.

There was also a very intricate system of transportation routes throughout Roman cities stretching to the distant corners of its ever-expanding empire. Inns and other hospitable businesses were constructed along these lines of passage to provide service to tired, weary, hungry, and thirsty travelers. Employees were then needed to tend to these travelers, and such was the beginning of the hospitality industry as we know it today. At that time, however, the employee did everything: receive the guest, take care of his things and tend to his horse if he had one, prepare a room, a bath, a meal, and most importantly, an alcoholic beverage.

Bartending's Present

The pay has never been as rewarding for drink slingers as it is today, and we are responsible for doing way less stuff to earn it. Nowadays, bartenders will even complain about having to run their own dirty dishes back to the dish pit, or roll their eyes when we have to walk around the perimeter of the bar to take care of a table after the cocktail server was done for the night. What can we say? It's a hard-knock life.

Since the days of Antiquity, the role of a bartender has evolved quite a bit. It didn't really become a gig you could make a decent living off of until the Europeans started settling in the new world and began setting up taverns and inns to accommodate the expanding presence of travelers, pioneers, and entrepreneurs. A lot of people got rich in a small amount of time, and most of them enjoyed going out and getting shitfaced.

In this day and age, bartending is most certainly a job that can pay the bills and then some. Bottom-of-the-barrel bartenders who work at places that are dead on a Friday night often make upwards of $20-30k per year. Those who are at the higher end of the spectrum, however, are known to make anywhere between $40-100k. You have to know your shit to make that kind of loot, though.

Bartending in All It's Glory

From what I've noted, most bartenders are simply passing by, stopping to make a quick buck while in route to something else. It's a very transient type of job with a humongous amount of turnover—perfect for someone who needs to work for a couple of months here and there either while traveling, going to school, running from the Feds, or opening a business of their own. Some stay for a few months, a few years, or even decades.

I've recently interviewed for several jobs outside of bartending (don't worry folks—just testing the water) and am often looked at with an expression of dismay or even pity when it comes to discussing my length of tenure at each company. What these suit-and-tie corporate zombies at human resources don't realize is that it is *very* rare for an employee in the hospitality industry to remain at the same joint for more than a couple years. Furthermore, they miss out on the concept that it's often better to jump from place to place.

Networking is something that I've learned a lot about while slinging drinks. While growing up, I always scoffed at the phrase "It's not what you know; it's *who* you know." I wanted to be the one who disproved all of that nepotism nonsense, but it's true in more cases than not. By bouncing around from bar to bar like a free-agent, not only do you learn new systems and menus, but you get to meet more people too.

Our professional schedules are really odd as well. "Days get shorter and shorter, nights get longer and longer. Before you know it, your life is just one long night with a few comatose daylight hours," Tom Cruise's character in the movie *Cocktail* so elegantly put it. That quote hits the nail on the head. The working hours of a bartender can be extremely fluky. Often, you're working the closing shift on a Saturday night, eventually getting home at 3am or later. After a few hours of shut-eye, you're right back at it in the morning to open the place, eyes crusted over and bloodshot, your whole body trembling from lack of sleep and too much caffeine.

Even though my father and uncles—all carpenters by trade—will probably call me a pussy for saying this, the physical toll that bartending takes on the body can be quite significant. It is a crime to sit down, and so you're on your feet all day. Over time, this can place a lot of strain on the knees and lower back. A crooked spine can also result from too many hours spent crouched over washing glasses in the tri-sink. These ailments are obviously background music compared to the damage that your liver is likely to take throughout your bartending tenure.

Even those who don't really drink that much will find themselves hugging the toilet more frequently now that they're behind the stick, as it sometimes proves impossible to turn down drinks or shots from your guests once you are seated on their side of the bar. And remember when I said that we make a pretty decent living given the working environment? Well, we have a way of spending it shortly after, too. That's right, we like to decompress every now and again, be it at the casino, a lavish dinner with friends, or a blurry night out at the local watering hole. And, we like tip our brothers and sisters-in-arms. We tip them a lot.

A Bartender's Identity

This is a tricky one. Just like the random collection of guests that gather at the pub to have a drink and socialize, those pouring the juice tend to come from many different walks of life. We vary on size and shape, from the 105 lb 23-year-old girl with sleeves of tattoos and ear gauges, to Art—a giant amongst men with a big, burly beard (his beard is so big that it has actually saved him from a concussion after a hard fall. We'll get to that story later).

Bartenders have all sorts of educational and professional backgrounds as well. I've worked with guys and gals who barely passed the GED exam, to those touting college degrees—including a doctorate. In fact, most bartenders that I've worked with *do* have college degrees of some sort —some even have two or three. I've served 'em up alongside present and future entrepreneurs, police officers, teachers, musicians, comedians, lawyers, and service members.

But make no mistake, folks. Just as there are a plethora of well-rounded drink slingers out there cranking away in bars and clubs across these great United States, there are also those who could hardly be labeled as model citizens. That's right—you know who you are, ya freaks. I speak of the addicts, and alcoholics—the bipolar, irresponsible, insomniacs feigning for a beer and a sloppy, meaningless one-nighter.

It's important to note, however, that these misfits could very well be the best ones. They are the true modern day pirates indulging in every moment, substance, and sexual organ that they can get their sweaty hands on. They get their guests drunk, and when their shift is over, they'll jump onto the other side of the bar to lessen the lead in the race. They tend to exhibit a superb knowledge of beers, wines, and libations, as they normally have at least trace amounts of either flowing through their bloodstream at any given moment. This breed of bartender is often unpredictable, hilariously fun, and always has a story to tell.

A Bartender's Sex Life

Incest. That is the word of the day, folks. Whether you wanted to know this or not, most of the single employees at the watering hole (and some of the taken ones) are all fucking each other.

Perhaps it's the environment in which we work—an emotionally-charged space crowded with hormonal mammals whose responsible decision-making capabilities diminish with each sip of booze. Or maybe all of the panty-dropping is correlated to the atypical schedules that restaurant employees work. We often sling drinks during random blocks of time that don't match up to those of potential mates who work traditional nine-to-fives. As a result, many just resort to banging those who are awake at the same strange hours of the day and night.

A Bartender's Sex Appeal

It's widely perceived that guests at the watering hole view whoever is pouring their drink as a sexier version of their off-duty persona. In other words, Betty appears to be a lot hotter when she's shaking a martini behind the bar than when you ran into her at the supermarket. Is this because the guy she's flirting and joking around with is on his fifth brewski? Have his beer goggles been activated? It appears that the host of the party (in this case it's Betty the bartender) has a higher social ranking than her shopping cart-pushing identity, undoubtedly because, as a bartender, she is the gatekeeper to something that the crowd wants: alcohol.

Dressed in nothing spectacular and wearing a minimal amount of makeup, she paces back and forth handing out drinks, change, compliments, and friendly insults. And in doing so, she has gained the sexual attraction of just about every guy seated at the bar. Some, under their breath, softly mutter to adjacent friends their desire to mate with her. Others make it known a bit more loudly and publicly. See the description of *The Creeper* in chapter four.

Would they be drooling and getting half-chubs in their pants if they bumped into Betty in the pasta isle at the nearest supermarket? Probably not. It's her swagger behind the bar, rather, that increases her sexual value. It's how comfortable and secure she seems as she interacts with complete strangers, her suave and delicate interaction with those who crave something gentle, and of course, her crude and blunt side that's capable of talking shit and taking shots with anyone. Most men (and many women) are hypnotized under her spell, yet she's just being herself—the same chick who you stood in line next to at Best Buy the day prior. She was hardly attention-grabbing then.

But screw yesterday—you long for her now! You are too nervous to say anything at first, so you have a few drinks to take the edge off. With each sip, another butterfly is killed-off inside of your belly. You inquire to those around you as you conduct an investigation to determine her eligibility. "Yo, bud—you know if she's got a boyfriend?" No one knows of such a person, so you decide to make a move.

The window of opportunity shrinks with each grain of sand that falls out of the hour glass. It's a bit later now—almost last call—and you're one of four people left at the bar. It's now or never, soldier.

"Hey, can I buy you a shot or something?"

"Aw, that's sweet of you honey. Sure. Want to do one with me?"

Boioioioioinngggg! The tent is pitched down below, and as both of you cheers and send your shots down the hatch, the words escape your mouth unhindered.

"Can I take you out sometime?"

Welp, that's it. There's no turning back now.

If she says no, she'll probably feel pretty weird the next time she sees you in the bar...or in the frozen section at the supermarket.

"Oh, I'm sorry. That's really sweet of you, but I have a boyfriend."

"Really? I thought maybe that you were interested since you took me up on that shot."

Ouch.

Look. Bartenders make their money on tips. If you're not interesting or attractive, we have to pretend like you are. It's all part of the experience. Some bartenders are admittedly straight-up hustlers, baiting guys and gals into investing in a possible future of hot, kinky sex by putting twenties into their tip jar. Others are simply genuinely nice and caring people—a personality trait that is often misinterpreted by guests as flirting. Such was the case with Betty and her not-so-secret admirer in this particular scenario.

Is all hope lost to bang that hot brunette behind the bar with all of the tattoos and piercings? Do bartenders ever hook-up with those whose bloodlines are not that of the restaurant nobility? Of course! In fact, if Betty had been going through a recent break-up, it's quite possible that she would have smuggled that guy through the kitchen and fucked him after hours in the walk-in. Like most things, it's a matter of circumstance.

It's important to note that, while at work, bartenders are surrounded by interesting people from all demographics of society. Additionally, we see a lot of wacky stuff and have heard just about every joke and pickup line at least twice. We can sniff out any malicious intent or fake asshole-ness like a drug detecting dog at the El Paso border. If you're really into the guy or gal that's serving you, your best bet is to be as genuinely nice and charming as possible, and to figure out a way of talking to them outside of the bar—aside from following them to their car or hiding outside of their bedroom window at night. Caught you, didn't I?!

On the other side of the coin, however, many drink slingers can be suckers for the siren—the mythological and seductive voice of pleasure that lures them to many bathroom stalls, apartment complexes, or back seats of cars to fool around after a night behind the bar. Bartenders are known to be absolute whores—both guys and gals. When they see someone that they want, they'll use their role to get paid and then get laid. It's practically a form of prostitution.

So how does a bartender land a piece of ass for the night? Sometimes, their tactics are looked at as genius by the surrounding natives, but it's often a ploy that's incredibly obvious and forthright. Maybe they'll buy a round for someone who they like. Or maybe they'll deploy a diversionary maneuver and flirt with someone directly next to their target to create a sentiment of jealousy. Then, when the time is right, they move in for the kill.

I've seen and executed some pretty incredible feats of fornication from behind the stick. It just so happens that normally, bar guests come to a bar to have a good time, and for that, bartenders often have an unfair advantage over the rest of the natives. It's unfair, I know. But it's simply because we are at the center of that good time.

From lengthy conversations and flirting, to up-front and brunt inquiries to fuck (such as 'Hi...Want to fuck?'), many bartenders have perfected the art of seduction from years of on-the-job training. Whilst slinging drinks, we are surrounded by sexual tension, and after spending a certain amount of time in this environment, it's easy to learn what to say and, more importantly—what *not* to say.

Bartenders Weigh-In On How To Find A Mate At The Watering Hole

It may sound a bit self-absorbed, but if you want to successfully find someone to mate with at the watering hole, become friends with the bartender first!

Whether or not it is your goal to land a life-partner or just someone to get naked with for the night, if you plan on conducting your hunt at the local bar, it's best to be on good terms with those who pour the drinks. On top of shaking martinis and taking food orders, bartenders engage in many activities that often go overlooked by the masses. Eavesdropping and matchmaking are good examples of such.

Over-serving a guest is a huge deal for us, and for that, we are always on high-alert for slurred speech and behavior that can prove to be dangerous, both to them, and to the rest of the frequenters at the drinking hole. We pace back and forth actively listening to the noises of the surrounding area, trying to get a bead on anything that should raise a red flag. But, in doing so, we often hear things that most of the room can't pick up on.

Want to know if the cute guy at the end of the bar is single? What is he drinking? Does he come here often? How big is the sausage in his...sandwich? These are all questions that the bartender can probably answer for you, *if*, of course, you are on good terms with him or her.

Matchmaking is another activity that comes with the job description. Economically, bartenders make more money on average if the guests are having a good time. It's rare that miserable or bored people tip well, and as a result, we like to stir the pot a bit. We're good at starting conversation and interaction amongst our guests who are unfamiliar with one another. We want you to succeed in your sexcapades, because if you fall flat on your face, you might end up scaring people away. If people leave due to you embarrassing yourself, we make less money. Therefore, we are actually inclined to help you.

Have your eyes set on the blonde across the bar? Well, it might behoove you to cozy-up to the bartender as a preemptive strike. Given that we're not in the weeds, we'll be glad to help you conduct a clandestine reconnaissance mission aimed at finding out if she's the type to slide her panties off on the first date. Like you'll soon read in the "A day in the life" chapter, you'd be surprised at how much of an effect being (or appearing like) chums with the bartender has on the others at the drinking hole.

If you are polite and courteous, tip well, and don't come off like a complete serial killer, I'd be happy to introduce you to her as "my good friend." She's been here quite a few times, and I have earned her trust. I've also noticed that she has at least three cocktails each visit. She's halfway through with her second one, so I suggest that we make a move now. I'll buy her next one on you, anonymously. Why anonymously? Because if I point across the bar at your goofy, bright-red face and say that it was you who bought the drink, she's likely to see that as a semi-pathetic move. She's attractive and gets drinks bought for her from all sides of the bar. You'd be nothing special—just another boring boob wearing an *Affliction* t-shirt.

With this prized target, we must be cunning and unorthodox. I will buy her a drink on your tab but will say that it's from a secret admirer (sounds corny, I know, but I've seen this work time and time again). Soon after, we will indirectly involve you in the interaction between the blonde and myself; perhaps we'll sit you down next to her and I introduce you as my friend. You have an *in* now, and it's up to you from here on out. I can help string you along, but if you pull any weird shit, I'll have to cover my own ass and start making excuses about why you're being creepy. *Ah, he gets like that sometimes when he hasn't had his meds.*

If you play your cards right, however, you can work-in the fact that you're the secret admirer once you get her to start warming up to you. She'll most likely see it as charming and creative—albeit a bit silly—but creative, nonetheless. This surprised and semi-impressed lady will probably give her phone number to you if you haven't said anything too strange yet, but as you close the deal, just try to refrain from chopping her up into little pieces and stuffing them in your wall, as you'll make me look pretty untrustworthy.

Follow These Simple Guidelines To Increase Your Chances Of Success

Guys: (Heterosexual)

- Don't wear too much cologne.

- Introduce yourself to the bartender and tip well—it doesn't have to be excessive, but don't you dare leave me 15% and ask me to help you with anything other than finding the exit.

- Smile big and smile often (But not an "I'm here to talk to you about Jesus" smile).

- Just like in business, you want to be the competitor that is doing something different and innovative. In a room full of peacocking, chest-thumping muscle-heads, be willing and ready to poke fun at your beer gut or your twenty-minute mile. In sales, it doesn't matter how amazing the product is as the prospective buyer isn't likely to buy it if they don't actually like *you*. You want to make your target laugh before all else.

- Don't go for the predictable and tired "Can I buy you a drink" opener right away. Again, establish yourself as different. Be yourself! If you are having fun watching the game, place a friendly bet with your target along the lines of "If this guy strikes out, I'll buy you a beer. If he doesn't, you buy me one. Deal?" Use your knowledge to purposely increase your odds of losing the bet. The goal is to buy her a drink but in a less-than-traditional way. It may even open up more lines of conversation with her being able to boast and brag a bit. On the ther hand, it's always nice to get a girl to buy you a drink, but it doesn't happen often. Play the odds.

- Find a way to involve the bartender. The bartender is the zookeeper and the host of this grandiose party. Use him or her to break-up any awkward silence between you and your target. Most bartenders (myself included) will be more than happy to help if it means you staying longer and buying (and tipping) more.

- Tip your bartender again. You never know when you'll need their help once more, or to cover your ass for any strange Freudian slips that may escape your lips.

- If you get shot down in a blaze of glory, respond with "Fine—I have to go take a shit anyway." Look, you've already lost, but by saying something completely unexpected and off-the-wall, it may actually reverse her decision and result in a layer of intrigue in you.

Girls: (Heterosexual)

- Tip your bartender. If you piss us off by being cheap, we'll do everything in our power to make sure you end the night sobbing into your pillow.

- Tip your bartender. Not to sound redundant, but women who act too hot for their own stilettos are a dime a dozen—a breed we're not impressed with. Just because every guy in the bar wants to buy you a drink in hopes of fucking you, it doesn't excuse you from the laws of the land. Plus, as you're probably already aware, there *is* an abundance of creepers out there. You want us on your side when he asks you to go home with him to help put the lotion in the basket.

- You'll most likely be the one who's being pursued, so just smile politely and say hello. Creepers are expecting a snarky response from the get-go, so being genuinely nice to them will catch them off-guard and briefly stun them.

- Enlist the help of the bartender if you are feeling uncomfortable. Just like for the guys, we want you to enjoy yourself so that you visit us often and spend money. If you catch someone staring at you from the other side of the bar while drooling on their NASCAR shirt and fingering their bellybutton, let us know so we can handle it. We won't hesitate to *86* someone if they threaten the sanctity of the watering hole.

- Let me be your boyfriend. Look, the fact of the matter is that men can get incredibly aggressive and creepy once they've had a few drinks and are on the hunt for punani. If you are out and don't want any solicitations whatsoever, I (we) can actually serve as your acting boyfriend/girlfriend for the night to deter any non-desirable company. Who knows—you may actually just want to sleep with me instead.

- Always, always, *always* keep an eye on your drink. You never know what that slobbering, bellybutton-fingering hillbilly is capable of.

Getting Out Alive

This is how many former bartenders look at walking away from the job. They snap out of the multi-year or multi-decade trance that they've been in and decide to hang-up their bottle poppers for reasons good and bad. Some quit because their liver just can't handle all of the "quality control," while others hang 'em up to chase the job of their dreams or the love of their life. Relationship stressors, kids, and jail time are also common reasons that bartenders leave the gig. Then, there are those who simply can't stand serving the public anymore.

Going home every night with your pockets stuffed with cash can be highly addictive—something that seems stupid to distance yourself from. But it's a job that rarely offers health benefits, steady pay (as some nights can leave you with $6 and others with $600), or even breaks during which to eat a protein bar. After years of living the odd life, many bartenders begin to yearn for what most of their friends and family have: some type of normalcy.

There are lifers, however. There are those who want nothing to do with normalcy. They love every second of being behind their sticky, corroded, wooden bar top and wouldn't trade it for the world. Eventually, they begin to take on roles in consulting or bar management, but only to ease-up a bit on their bodies. They'll pour beers and talk shit with their regulars until someone pries their bottle openers from their cold, lifeless fingers. They'll die bartending in all of its glory.

3

Watering Holes

I've studied the world's most complex and obscure fauna on all seven continents during my time as a zoologist, but none as fascinating as the drunken human being. The battle at Kruger National Park is bollocks compared to watching a brawl between two beer-league softball players at the neighborhood bar and grill. As entertaining as it is to witness a crocodile play tug-o-war against a lion while using a baby water buffalo as the rope, it holds no candle to watching two grown alpha talking-monkeys duke it out after too many shots of bourbon.

The funny thing is, they'll likely end up playing rock-paper-scissors over cab fare as they hug it out and make up a few minutes later.

I remember sitting in the Department of Motor Vehicles thinking about how interesting it would be to film a documentary there. Such drama! Cave creatures that make Tolkien's Gollum look like a bronzed, ripped actor from Baywatch fending off angry and impatient men and soccer moms in desperate pursuit of driver's licenses. The body odor, the yelling, the screaming, the coughing, the farting, *the snoring, the booger-picking—all of it would make for great footage.*

It seems as though, however, that I stumbled upon a project with much more drama wrapped-up in it than the DMV: The human watering hole. The indigenous arrived in droves to stand in a crowded room with a sticky floor covered in peanut shells and pilsner. I was determined to find out why.

***

So, have you ever *really* thought about why you end up at a bar? Walking into the local saloon is something that many of us do quite regularly and without really giving it much thought. The most common answer, of course, is for socialization purposes. Most of us barge into the local drinking establishment to embed ourselves in the company of others.

Even if someone has no interest in speaking to another human, they still find themselves craving the sensation of the covalent bond that occurs when human beings share the atmosphere. Droves of folks leave their living quarters and arrive at the bar to step foot into a stimulating environment and to enjoy a drink. They want to be a part of the herd even if they enjoy being on the outskirts.

Social interaction is so imperative to the evolution of the human psyche that, without it, the majority of us will literally go insane. Take prison life, for example: if you screw up too often while already behind bars, your punishment is to be removed from the other inmates and placed in solitary confinement.

As much as we love our alone time, too much alone time can be unhealthy. There are exceptions, of course. The bearded man on the mountain whose only interaction comes in the form of his pet skunk seems to be doing just fine. But instinctively, we humans are pack animals. Some seem destined to break away from the pack and take for the hills. But for the most part, I need you and you need me.

We parade into our local bars to rub elbows with others in our tribe and those from other tribes. Boredom, sadness, excitement, loneliness, being horny—these are all emotions and sensations that direct us to the bar for a drinky-drink. Simply put, the bar is the best venue our adult species has to socialize. Kids have the playground, teenagers have the mall, and adults have the watering hole.

Appealing to the Senses

There aren't many man-made environments or dwellings that are more enticing and appealing to our senses than the barroom. The sights, sounds, and the bustling energy of a busy night in the front of the house are what subconsciously tickle our sensibilities and reel us in through the entrance.

Sometimes, while at the bar either working or playing, I close my eyes and just listen to the sweet sounds of a Saturday night at the bar—the crashing noise of side plates being stacked, the clinking of wine glasses, the tinkling of a freshly tumbled cocktail as the bartender unleashes it into a sparkling Collins glass, the hypnotic vibration of the house jazz band's drummer's snare, the isolated and sporadic eruptions of laughter scattered throughout the room—it all comes together as a beautiful and harmonic symphony of the interaction amongst friends and strangers alike. Mozart couldn't have done better if he tried.

Pick a Hole, Any Hole

So, you want to go out but aren't exactly sure which type of bar is best suited to fit your agenda. Where's the best place for a quick pint and a boxing debate? How about a good spot for live music? Trying to find skanks? What if you're wearing board shorts? What are the best types of spots for visitors flying solo?

Every drinking hole has its own theme, personality, and attracts all sorts of different demographics of guests, so you'll need to come to a conclusion over the most appropriate venue to suit your wants and needs. Here is a brief summary of a few of the most popular types of arenas frequented by drinking, talking monkeys.

Chains

I experienced some sort of Déjà vu when I entered the chain restaurant. It's like I had been there before even though I know that I hadn't. The lighting, the sounds, the smells, the dress of the employees—even the menu; it all seemed very familiar to me.

***

When Willy stumbled into the local chain restaurant/bar, he entered into an environment that is the product of much collaboration between statisticians, accountants, consultants, psychologists, and marketing gurus. A chain or franchise usually starts with one successful shop that becomes a model for expansion. One becomes three. Three becomes forty. Forty becomes hundreds. They multiply like horny rabbits.

Chains like Red Lobster, Outback Steakhouse, Hooters, and TGI Fridays, are tightly-run ships that specialize in efficiency and the planned recidivism of its customers. The menus are designed using market trends, as well as psychological and behavioral information, such as where and why a guest's eyes focus the most. The ambience of Applebee's is meticulously designed to make visitors in Oregon feel like their eatin' good in their own neighborhood of Anytown, USA.

Now, I'm not a snob of chain restaurants by any means. Having said that, there tends to be less emphasis on personality in the job description for a server or bartender at Ruby Tuesday and more on professionalism, proficiency, and lack of felonies. As in any corporate structure, these types of establishments tend to have long chains of command and absolutely no tolerance for bullshit. They'll ax you for not taking your earrings out before a shift without batting an eye. I wouldn't necessarily say that employees of chains are expendable, but perhaps easily replaceable.

Anyway, I haven't personally had any experience as a chain restaurant employee. I think it would be like going back to boot camp after so much time spent working in small business. Chains are successful because they have decent, reasonably-priced grub and overall competent service. It's a comfortable atmosphere because it's familiar and crafted to stimulate the senses with novelty doodads and decorations inspired by local flora and fauna. They do a good job of making you feel at home no matter where you happen to be.

Chains are also great places to eat on a budget. These cookie-cutter businesses are normally located near office complexes or within a short distance to a corporate center. They offer a quick, fulfilling, inexpensive, and informal lunch or after-work destination to plan the next marketing project or how you and another conspirator plan on blowing up Lumbergh's office.

The bussers, servers, bartenders, and low-level management deal with a lot of bullshit to earn their keep at a chain restaurant. They're all at high-risk of being exposed to soul-sucking micromanagement phrases such as "the difference between ordinary and extraordinary is that little extra." And similar to Peter's rant to the Bobs in the movie *Office Space*, if you make a mistake, whether it be accidentally firing a table's clams only seconds after you send their hummus, or forgetting to wear your shitty tie to work, you're likely to hear it from several different bosses.

Also, if a chain restaurant is where you make a living, you'll have to do so under steady infiltration by secret shoppers (the cunty spies of the culinary business model that will make a stink about something stupid on purpose just to see how the employees react). If you can work through all of that, a steady clientele base and plenty of opportunities to advance up the corporate ladder (if you so dare) shall be your reward.

At corporate, every seat represents a closely estimated figure of yearly revenue. For example, it could be said that the average monthly gain from one barstool is $2,000. That would make the yearly expected revenue $24,000 for that one barstool. The importance of sustaining those figures in such a closely measured manner tends to make for a mechanized dining experience.

You probably won't be served as many shots of whiskey or enjoy the dirty jokes that you would at the local dive bar. And it's not the right place to ask the bartender to play your favorite Kesha song, as the music will be just loud enough to notice but not loud enough to groove to. However, the odds are that your lunch or dinner service will be efficient, enjoyable, and convenient enough for you to not rule-out a return visit.

Dives

I've never seen so many creatures asleep around one watering hole at the same time. Those who were actually awake and conscious swatted flies away from their drinks and paraded back and forth to the exit to smoke cigarettes, stopping only to feed money into the music box.

Everyone seemed to know everyone else by first and last name. I've learned that most of this spot's inhabitants frequent it almost every day at about the same time each day. Just about everyone had a pseudonym or nickname or their own designated barstool. The socializing was low to moderate during the daytime hours but became excessively loud and rambunctious after sundown.

The locals weren't exactly standoffish, but I was a new face and they seemed to be curious of me. I paid my respects and made a comment or two about a hard day's work on the job, escaping the nagging broad at home, or the local sports team, and I was in. My backside was numb from my shoddy barstool, my pint glass smelled like an anus, and my elbow kept sticking to the wooden bar top. One might ask themselves why anyone would want to come to a place like this. I don't why, but I fell in love with it quite quickly!

***

"I don't enjoy dive bars," said no decent person ever.

If you don't love a good dive bar, you have no soul. You are a shallow and hopelessly tasteless blob of tissue who has falsely convinced yourself that you're better than cheap beer, stale bar snacks, and fart jokes.

This is the land of the real. Dives are the preferred hangout for the average hardworking American citizen, including the deranged bartender who just stirred your $15 dollar Manhattan at the stuffy, snobby martini lounge adjacent to the corporate complex down the street you just got done kissing ass at.

Neighborhood dive bars usually include a *who's who* array of local celebrities. When you push the door open and allow some light into the room, you're likely to spot the town mechanic, the mailman, the all-state home run hero who almost made the pros, and the retired school principal, among many other wholesome and down-to-earth folk.

Dives are often unimpressive spaces that boast the most impressive examples of loyal patronage. Some people that I've talked with have proudly claimed to have been drinking at the same dive for over forty years.

It's an environment that has become a vital staple in the lives of the natives. It's where many quench their thirst before, during, and after the workday. Their local watering hole has given them many late nights and painful mornings, and almost certainly some scarring of their livers. It's where drunken dreams to rule the world are born, and where harsh reality lays those dreams to rest years later.

If you're in the mood for simplicity sprinkled with a little friendly crudeness, you'll feel right at home at a dive bar. Dives can be great destinations at any point during a night out, whether as the first stop, the main stop, or the last stop.

Dressed in mud-covered construction attire, a beer league softball uniform, or an elegant opera gown, it matters not, for you'll be greeted with a smile, a semi-cold beer in a semi-clean glass, and an unassuming and welcoming "How ya doin?" Leave your drama and materialistic side at the door, for these barroom heroes will more likely be impressed by how fast you can chug a beer rather than how expensive your boat is.

Smile, be friendly, pull-up a barstool, and don't complain about the fly that made its way into your drink. Just scoop it out, hold up your glass, and cheers to the best bar you've ever made your way into.

Beach Bars

This was quite simply the most fun I've seen people have at the watering hole. Everyone was half-naked, bronzed, and becoming quite intoxicated indeed. The drinks were colorful, and the evidence of plastic surgery bounced up and down all over the place.

At this particular spot located at the New Jersey shore, I witnessed packs of loud, imposing, hairy, primate-looking creatures—referred to by the locals as 'Guidos' or 'Bennys'—

grinding their genitalia on their targeted mates while the sun was highest in the sky. It was very odd in terms of mating rituals, being that most of the mating I've documented in humans either happens very early or very late in the day.

I've also learned that I'm not the first one to study these bipedals in this particular setting. Several years back, a group of sociologists filmed a prolonged documentary titled 'The Jersey Shore' which followed this often violent tribe in grand detail, filming their every hump and vomit for several seasons. Furthermore, they even resembled the families of warring chimps that I covered a decade ago deep in the bush of Africa. But aside from the 'Benny,' there are many other types of visitors that enjoy the festive atmosphere of the beach bar.

Everyone seemed to enjoy themselves here more than at the other places. It could have been a combination of the mood-enhancing vitamins they were absorbing from the sun, the cold alcohol that doused everyone's thirst on such an unbearably hot day, or the fact that most visitors here seemed to be free from their responsibilities for several days. Perhaps it was a combination of all three.

* * *

Normally, folks at the tiki hut standing alongside the water are in a more relaxed and mellow state of mind than, say, people at a bar in downtown Cincinnati. Why's that? Well, these coastal drinking establishments typically serve as a socializing point for hoards of hardworking people that are on some sort of vacation—temporary or permanent—and who are looking to leave their worries on the mainland.

They're overworked, underpaid, and have at least a year's worth of built-up thirst for salted margaritas and rum daiquiris.

The ambience is carefully designed to assist you in your conquest to silence the echoing voice of your nagging boss. The bartenders also help mitigate this meditative transformation as they sloppily overfill your plastic cup with your favorite liquid remedy. The hypnotic beats of reggae music paired with the sound of crashing waves massage your ear canals until you can't help but breathe in deeply and smile.

When you're on the water, you're literally at the end of livable space—unless, of course, you live on a boat. There's a reason surfers always seem so happy and fulfilled with life, even if they end up riding their rusted-out bicycle back home to their cardboard box after a dawn patrol session. And no, the sweet ganja herb isn't *solely* responsible for all of that joy and Zen-like state of mind.

It's because they spend their leisure time literally looking out at nothing. They float on their boards, waiting for the next wave to roll through, all doing so at the end of their own world and the entrance to an alien, aquatic one. It's tranquil. It's deep. It's profound and thought-provoking.

But for those 9-5'ers-turned-pirates for a week drinking frozen cocktails and ripping shots of tequila at the straw-roofed bar up the beach, the ecosystem of this kind of place promotes happiness itself. The positive vibes gyrating through the speakers hidden in palm leaves, as well as the buzz the frequenters get off of their bartender-prescribed amnesia meds have them feeling quite Zen-like as well, and without the threat of shark attacks.

Beach bars are fun. And they're fun to work at too. Just due to sheer volume, a bartender at a half-decent beach bar can make thousands upon thousands of greenbacks in a given three-month span during the summer. The best spots are enjoyed by those of all ages, playing host to young and ripped college athletes dancing drunkenly with 60-year old ladies in one-pieces to the sounds of the house band.

Old and young money set up shop early in the season to establish their regularity. Hooking-up tends to be easier here than at most spots, barring a dark nightclub filled with horny fist pumpers on Molly.

I challenge you to go to a beach bar and not have a good time. Even if your girlfriend left you and you lost your job and your truck broke down and your dog died—fuck it! There's bound to be a plethora of attractive people who love making bad decisions. Also, no one has a job on this particular day, and you won't need a truck to get home after you pass out on a pool chair for the night. No worries allowed here. Just enjoy yourself. And tip your bartender.

Irish Pubs

They talked funnier in this environment than I do! The Irish pub was rustic and cozy. Most of this dwelling was constructed from some type of dark, sturdy wood. Most of those seated on the barstools were drinking a dark, liquid alcohol that looked black in the dim lighting of the area.

The noise level was fairly low, but I did here a local frequenter say that this particular drinking hole can become quite chaotic indeed. It's a comfortable spot—almost reminiscent of a hobbit hole that could be found in the shire. Its frequenters include the young, the elderly, loners, and families alike.

***

It's commonly known that the Irish pubs we're familiar with in the United States were originally designed to play host to Irish immigrants that traversed the Atlantic in search of a better life in the new world. It was a place to run to after a long day of enduring harsh working conditions, as well as to enjoy a traditional bowl o' stew and a pint o' brew.

A good Irish pub is the epitome of a community staple. The concept began as a metaphorical tree fort for all of the grownups of the local Irish population in cities like New York, Boston, and Philadelphia. Once inside, they were free to speak their minds, eat the food that they grew up eating, and to sing rebel songs. The pub was a mold of the corner pub back on the Emerald Isle that provided a comfortable and cozy taste of home.

It's important to note, however, that there are droves of bars that throw a shamrock on the wall, install a Guinness tap, name themselves something generic like O'Neil's, Murphy's, or McNamara's, and undeservedly declare themselves an Irish pub. But if there are real Irish people sitting on the barstools, then it's good Irish pub to be at.

The ambience of an Irish pub is normally quite homely. While bartending in an Irish pub for several years, I always found it to be the coziest and most intimate of the establishments in which I've worked. My personal lineage is mostly made up of keg-tossing, telephone pole-throwing, kilt-wearing Scotsmen, but the fact is that the Irish and the Scottish are very similar in terms of their respective exoduses across the ocean. They have a sense of pride that will match any tribe of people, and they hold onto their roots like the last fat kid in a tug o' war match reluctantly being drug across the finish line.

It's common, on the dark, wooden walls, to see an attic's worth of old family photographs, newspaper clippings from the old country, antique burlap potato sacks, and depending on where the owner's loyalties lay, possibly a dartboard with a less-than-flattering picture of the Queen fastened across the target area.

The sights, the sounds, and the faire are all meant to actualize the Irish lifestyle and experience. The meticulously-crafted perfect pint of Guinness, all of the dusty photos and knickknacks that hang around the room, the soft voices singing rebel and sailing songs that mist through the sound system, or even a live musical set with local Irish personalities leading the way, all paint a vivid and nostalgic picture of the life that they left behind across the Atlantic.

As much as these beloved establishments serve as homes away from home for many Irish, Scottish, and even English folk alike, they proudly welcome those from any and all backgrounds to enjoy their ancestors' recipe of shepherd's pie and a glass of an almost endless selection of aged whiskey. I've served Sicilians, Nigerians, Greeks, French, Welsh, Puerto Ricans, Spaniards, Germans, Romanians, Japanese, Guatemalans, and many other travelers while working in an Irish pub. It seems that these particular watering holes act as the United Nations of the restaurant world.

I love a good Irish pub and armies of people from all backgrounds do too. As well as dives, these comfortable abodes are centered around family and tradition. I have to say that, while slinging drinks behind the bar at one of these dwellings, there have certainly been moments where I imagined my late grandfather who hailed from Glasgow sitting at my bar and enjoying a drink and some homemade traditional stew, humming away to songs he grew up singing, his eyes scanning black and white images of shipping docks or pubs from back home that are strewn across the bar, the ol' brute in a trance of contemplation and nostalgia of the decision he made to jump on a boat and cross an ocean in search of something else many years prior.

The Club

Well, I couldn't see a bloody thing so I didn't write many notes. I couldn't hear at all so a voice recorder was out. As a result, this report is based off of sheer memory—and that's awfully faded and shaky from all of the ecstasy I ate.

I felt like I was in a Stanley Kubrick movie or something. For several hours, I lived my life in short, fragmented slides under the low glow of pulsating strobe lights. The noise shook my inner bones as the repetitious and rhythmic blasts hypnotized my fists into pumping up and down all night.

The place smelled like un-wiped assholes, sweat, and Red Bull. I was flat broke after paying the entrance fee and buying a few drinks, and I assume that I swapped spit with at least one person being that I had lipstick marks on my face and woke up with a piece of gum in mouth that wasn't originally mine.

It's a mad world, but a fun one. I remember laughing hysterically and being in awe of the unified sea of arms waving to the inducing and shocking pulses of sound, which I imagined was the collision of Norwegian, German, and Swedish beat-boxing robots.

I feel like absolute shit. My head hurts. My eyes sting. I vomited twice today. I maxed out my credit card after buying five shots of tequila. My ears are ringing. I feel dumb, and I'm missing random pieces of clothing—including my skivvies. The blur of it all left me with many questions and very few answers...

***

I've had my fair share of long nights and confusing mornings after a trek out to the club—both domestically and internationally. Heading to the club is not like stopping into the local bar for a drink or two. It's a commitment. Unless you're the saint that's willing to behave in order to care for and drive the sinners home, you're not going to be in the condition to commute anywhere after the fact. You're not paying an arm and a leg to just step foot into the room to take it easy, to discuss the upcoming golf event, or to network for your interior design business. You're there to rage.

If your grandparents happened to catch a glimpse of what you were up to—pupils wide as frisbees and sweating profusely from the several uppers you ingested, dry humping and making out with someone you met 90 seconds prior, ripping shots of overpriced rubbing alcohol at the bar, and throwing your arms up and down in unison alongside an overcrowded hoard of dancing zombies—they'd probably shake their heads in disapproval.

Perhaps the shame or embarrassment element is why this type of watering hole is always kept so dark and loud—it's that much harder to realize that you're most likely making a laundry list of bad decisions. If we were showed, in high definition, a replay of exactly what we were up to while Afrojack's mash-ups charmed us into such a wildly-energetic trance, we would most likely have lots of material to laugh at and be grossed-out by. But in reality, the squished-in pack of drunken, hallucinating, slobbering clubbers makes for one hell of a sample for sociological and psychological study.

You see a lot of interesting behavior when you grace the floor of the hottest club in town. I think it's safe to say that your inner-primate has a better chance of showing itself at a place like this, more so than at a martini lounge or chain restaurant. Promiscuous sexual conduct, fights, insecurities —all of it has a home here.

Once past the SWAT-like security personnel, it's game on. Straight to the bar you march, because if not, that little mediating voice in the back of your head in the form of your inhibition will probably try to make you turn back. Everyone seems to be on the same level—the "I don't give a fuck" level. This is the right frame of mind to be in, honestly. It's the appropriate venue to be wild, mostly because that's the attitude that mostly everyone else has. Who can be judgmental and critical of your grotesque choice of a partner for a sloppy, two-hour groping and dry-humping clinic when all of your friends are doing the same exact thing just inches from you? If you don't tell, I won't.

Everyone should go ape-shit at a nightclub at least once. Why? Because if not, you'll miss out on the ritual of dressing-up together in the hotel room with friends while pounding shots of cheap booze, then jumping around and pumping your fists in harmony with hundreds to thousands of other buzzed party animals, sloppily making out with someone you find attractive (under the circumstances, at least), eating the greasiest food you can get your paws on after the fact, and eventually waking up in the same clothes that you had on when you had your first Red Bull and vodka —minus a sock, an earring, and maybe your undergarments.

Piecing the night back together and figuring out how to get back to your wolf pack is always a challenging quest that normally ends up as a great story to tell. It's an adventure to be had, so long as you ignore the sky-high cover charge, the asinine prices for drinks, and the inevitable damage to your hearing (and possibly your ego.)

Upscale

Of all the bars I've visited for my research, I was gawked at here the most. Apparently my khaki shorts, half-unbuttoned safari shirt, swamp boots, and safari hat didn't constitute as acceptable lounge attire. The natives here were all very well-groomed and didn't smell of that mixture of sweat and vomit like those at the nightclub. The ages at this drinking hole ranged greatly from young to old. The goods were definitely a bit more expensive, and the food portions were extremely tiny, as if they were fixin' on serving smurfs.

In terms of noise, there was some laughter but no yelling—just lots of business talk and some ranting about politics and the economy. In this place, after exploring the other types of watering holes, I couldn't help but feel how I did when I was given the so-called honor of sitting at the adult table during large family gatherings: bored, uninterested, and reminiscent of my time spent engaged in food fights and making fart noises with my armpit. After about an hour of observation at this drinking hole, I wanted to go back to the dive...

* * *

As expected, Willy didn't feel too comfortable in such a fancy establishment. Upscale means expensive. Expensive means exclusive. Exclusive means no riffraff. And being that our nature expert has, at times, been labeled as a bit of a scallywag, I wasn't expecting him to feel too at home here.

It's interpreted by many as a place of sophistication. The food, the drink, the clientele—all suave and cultured. A martini lounge or wine bar may not be the most exciting place to park your bum, but it is nice destination to unwind, collect yourself, and enjoy a little taste of the good life.

Cheeseboards, Spanish and French wines, aged Scotches, and neatly rolled linens combine to make the upscale lounge a comfortable venue to meet with friends, family, and colleagues, free, of course, from 12 year-old little demons in soccer uniforms flicking food and boogers at each other while their parents remain (or pretend to be) oblivious.

Just as first-class or business-class airfare keeps you protected (except from those like myself who enjoy crop-dusting the first-class cabin while boarding) from the wide range of possible annoyances that can present themselves during a flight, paying higher prices and having to adhere to a dress code all but ensures that you'll be safe from those who are likely to be classified as "non-desirables."

This works out very well for women, as there tend to be less creepers. The dive bar creeper will be of no worry to you here, and I doubt you'll encounter any solicitations like "Hey...umm...you got a purdy mouth...you wanna come up to my apartment tonight? I live upstairs, and I'm sure JimBob won't mind you bein' there much. There's a Duck Dynasty marathon on the TV later..."

I'll admit, I do on occasion enjoy a nice, quiet place to sip on a painfully-overpriced glass of wine and nibble on some unimpressive and costly cheese. Why? I don't know. Maybe we enjoy these places because we're hoping to feel better about ourselves—like we made it into the admirals club or something. Just don't let your head get too big, or you'll be plummeting back down to Earth when you eventually pay your tab and climb back into your Toyota Corolla to head home.

4

The Drink

There was a sudden change in behavior in most of the frequenters once they ingested the drink. It was clear that some consumed more than others, which then seemed to have an obvious correlation to the severity of their actions. With each swig, some displayed an increase of friendliness, while others showed a surge of aggressive tendencies. A select few wanted to hump everything in sight.

As consumption continued amongst the frequenters, I saw more swapping of saliva and heard more burping. The watering hole quickly became louder and more unpredictable. Articles of clothing were lost. Chests were beaten and fists were thrown. Hugs were given. Tears streamed down faces and vomit was projected onto the floor. Some fell asleep while others simply fell.

***

If human beings are good at anything, it's finding ways to self-destruct. The drink that Willy witnessed the crowd at that watering hole putting into their bodies was alcohol. Simply put, alcohol is poison. Weird, right?

More specifically known as ethanol, this flammable and colorless liquid is the ingredient mainly responsible for much of the brilliance and flaws of human kind—not to mention countless of unplanned pregnancies. It can be consumed orally or anally and is enjoyed by people from all over the world.

Alternatively referred to as *booze, grog, juice, sauce, firewater*, and *the white man's burden*, alcohol has been finding its way into our bloodstreams since ancient times. In fact, the ancient Sumerians (now modern-day Iraqis) used to toast to the goddess of alcohol, the beautiful Ninkasi, as they slurped on whatever they liked to slurp on back then. Furthermore, convincing evidence out of the orient points to people getting wasted on alcohol for as far back as 9,000 years ago.

Thank Ninkasi that someone figured it out! To spare you all of the chemistry jargon (and frankly, to spare myself as I hated high-school chemistry), the alcohol that we put into our bodies via shot glasses and beer funnels is created by the process of fermentation. What's that? Basically, it's the combining of sugars and yeast. The two ingredients flirt with each other, mate, and eventually consumable alcohol is born.

So why would someone want to put poison into their body? Just ask any hardworking "Joe," musician, writer, comedian, or even remotely interesting person that you can find. It's because we are aware of ourselves (at least most of us are). Life presents us with a lot of pain and uncertainty about our existence, and the effects that alcohol have on the body can temporarily make you feel a whole lot better about almost anything. Whether you're living the lyrics of a depressing country song or just need to break away from your nine-to-five identity, introducing some firewater into your bloodstream is a popular way of self-medicating that can be much cheaper than going to see a shrink.

How does alcohol work? How does it get us drunk? Well, like mentioned earlier, *most* ingest alcohol orally. I say most because there are nuts out there who prefer soaking tampons in vodka or whiskey and shoving them up their assholes. This method will get you drunk faster because your intestines absorb liquid quicker than your stomach does. But for traditionalists such as myself, wrapping our lips around a pint glass or bottle and drinking it is how the magic begins.

Once it flows refreshingly down your throat (or glops down if you've been tricked into shooting a cement mixer), it ends up in the gut. From there, it seeps into the bloodstream and is then filtered by the liver before finding its way into the toilet—or more commonly—onto the toilet *seat*. Alcohol, once introduced into the body, begins to depress the central nervous system which attributes to various slowing and debilitating effects in the arena of coordination, cognitive function, and important bodily functions...like getting a boner.

The problem with alcohol consumption is that, in small doses, it's often euphoric. Why is euphoria a problem? Because humans are greedy little piggies, of course. We gorge and guzzle all that we can, often until our stomachs expand to the level of physical pain. We portray the same gluttonous tendencies when it comes to emotions, too. When you start to feel that amazing tickling sensation that follows a few sips of your favorite beer after a long day of yard work, you want it to last. Most people drink more and drink faster in hopes of prolonging the feeling of being all gooey and wonderful inside.

It's a valiant effort, but this strategy is actually counter-productive. I'm sorry to be a party-pooper here, but once you're at that initial level of euphoria, it's literally not going to get better than that. But, you ask, what about how happy we become when we're one-eye-shut drunk and our favorite hockey team wins the game in triple-overtime? Or what about the phone number you get at last call—that's a happy moment, right? Yes, of course. If you're in the bathroom puking your brains out and someone runs in screaming to inform you that you ended up winning the Powerball lottery that night, you won't let a few dangling beads of acidic snot dripping from your nose ruin your celebratory dance, would you?

Aside from watching your team win, getting a sexual favor in parking lot, or winning the lottery, your dopamine levels are highest just after ingesting a small amount of booze. You're not drunk yet—you're just buzzed. Once you start wandering past this land of happy hugs and epiphanies, however, you'll start to notice that the terrain gets harder to navigate. You begin to lose your balance and trip over things as the ground becomes unstable. Objects start to appear out of nowhere as you unavoidably smash into them. The lack of oxygen traveling to your brain results in slowed thinking and speech. Soon, you'll enter a wormhole that will deliver you to the restroom where you'll pass out on the toilet after an exorcism of bodily fluids and solids from both ends.

Prohibition

Your history teachers probably left this part out of the lesson plan, but alcohol has played an immeasurably important role in the formation of the world as we know it.

In his recent special *How Booze Built America,* beloved television host Mike Rowe divulges that the pilgrims only landed at Plymouth Rock simply because they had run out of beer. Apparently they were originally headed further south and decided to stop and assess their shortages. Mike also tells us that John Wilkes Booth—the guy who shot Abraham Lincoln at the Ford's Theater—was getting all looped-up at the bar downstairs before heading up to pull the trigger. Among other hypothetical questions, the host of *Dirty Jobs* wonders if Booth would have done it if he didn't fill himself up with liquid courage before-hand. It's an interesting discussion to be had.

And then came prohibition...

The whole debacle began in the early 1900s as an attempt to curtail the amount of crime that the government—in typical American fashion—blamed on the increased numerical presence of immigrants throughout the country's cities. The prohibitionist and all-around good vibe-murderer Clinton N. Howard was quoted declaring that alcohol enthusiasts were "Laying with the boys and bums, spending their money debauching their characters, rotting their bodies, and jeopardizing their immortal souls." Wait—you mean all of the fun stuff, right? I mean, who doesn't love a little soul jeopardizing every now and then?

C'mon Howard, lighten up. Yeah, I guess alcohol abuse was on the rise since the revolution and more and more accidents were occurring in the workplace due to drunkenness, but is completely attacking and outlawing something the best course to take? If you're a FOX News loyalist who believes that the United States is winning the war on drugs, go ahead and nod your head yes. Everyone else—well, you get the idea.

Of course, as with most trending social issues, the two opposing sides of the argument detracted further and further away from each other. Religious groups inevitably got involved which resulted in the forming of the *drys* and the *wets*. I bet you've already figured out which side lobbied in favor of what. I mean, generally speaking, when the hell is the word "dry" ever used to describe something good? Wines, maybe. But like Steve Miller sang in his band's hymn *Jungle Love,* "Everything's better when wet!"

The shit really hit the fan when the 18th amendment was passed in 1919 which would eventually make the manufacture and sale of alcohol illegal and highly punishable —the key word being *eventually* (it's important to note that prohibition wasn't enforced yet. It was only a draft at this time). It was silly for those legislators to think that a nation formed by rebels was not going to rebel against this war on fun.

Booze then became officially illegal which consequently brought about the genocide of perfectly-crafted ales, whiskeys, and wines. Good folk could only watch as lawmen smashed open countless bottles and barrels of their favorite firewater, the streams of goodness bleeding out onto the ground and being absorbed by mother earth. Something had to be done, damnit.

Ever hear of the *Volstead Act?* Well, this itty-bitty piece of legislation (or lack thereof) stated that anything with an alcohol by volume (abv) rating of 5% or higher was now to be considered officially illegal. It also went as far as outlawing any type of machinery that was used to manufacture alcohol. The Volstead act is what officially authorized the actual enforcement of prohibition legislation. Luckily, the government screwed-up when they signed it into play.

One has to wonder whether or not the authors of this law were actually drunk themselves when their pens hit paper. I mean, they kind of left out the part about the actual consumption of alcohol. And also, since the act went into effect a year after the amendment was passed, everyone who already possessed legally-purchased alcohol was grandfathered in. These people were free to indulge themselves in their own private quarters as long as they were not selling it to others—unless of course you had a doctor who was willing to write you a permission slip to buy it. It just so happened that the act allowed for consumption if it was prescribed for medical purposes.

Speakeasies (secret, clandestine bars and taverns—the original ones, not the hipster hangouts we are familiar with today) were born when demand surged past the available supply. All of those cases of liquor that were legally purchased before the Volstead Act were pounded and chugged all too quickly, leaving the drinker with no drink. Enter Al Capone and others like him.

This Chicago based entrepreneur and his cronies hired importing specialists—sometimes referred to as "rum runners"—to smuggle rum into the country to be sold at these secret bars. They also contracted people to smuggle whiskey in from Canada. With the supply of alcohol restored and the birth of discreet watering holes in which to drink and socialize, it goes without saying that these gangsters probably had a significantly higher approval rating than the fools who enacted the prohibition law.

Good finally whooped evil's ass in 1933 with the ratification of the 21st amendment, which in turn repealed the 18th amendment. The growing hatred for the policy by common citizens, paired with the infamous crash of the stock market in 1929 that triggered the great depression, amounted to be enough to change the minds of the government concerning alcohol. The country was broke and booze was the business boom that it needed. I won't dare say that the government learned its lesson to stay the hell out of the private citizen's business when it comes to consumption, simply because in the year 2014, marijuana is still illegal in more places than not.

It's quite noteworthy that, for the first and *only* time in our nation's history, an amendment was fully repealed. I guess beer muscles can prove to be a good thing every now and then.

One Final Thought: Alcohol

Like stated earlier, simply put, alcohol is poison. But it's very special poison. It's a truth serum. It invigorates us and then debilitates us; is the problem and the solution. It helps us celebrate as well as mourn. It's a lucrative business for some and a money pit for others. But regardless, a little firewater sure does make life more interesting.

Eliminate alcohol from the history books and you might as well toss along with it stacks of the most influential art and cultural achievements ever known to man. Van Gogh, Hemmingway, Churchill—they all found themselves at the bottom of countless bottles of their preferred rye. Who knows how dull life would be without the delicious, liver-corroding toxin we call alcohol? After all, it was Benjamin Franklin who, in a letter to André Morellet in 1779, wrote "Behold the rain which descends from heaven upon our vineyards, there it enters the roots of the vines, to be changed into wine, a constant proof that God loves us, and loves to see us happy."

5

The Natives

I was nervous to begin this project at first—even more so than I've been before a solo expedition into the Amazon or the mountains of New Zealand. It had been quite some time since I had been in the company of people—especially complete strangers. I knew that it would be important to internalize the customs and actual environment of the local drinking hole, but the whole study would rely on how well Jay and I captured the fauna. I puked on the helicopter insertion.

As a guest in their ecosystem, I was to roam the confines of the grounds in search of exotic and fascinating bar frequenters and bartenders—all in a fairly small window of time. Get in, meet some interesting people, and then get out. That was the mission, and I think I succeeded.

During my observational period of the bipedal drinking establishment, I documented some very unique characters— ones that I'll surely never forget. This segment of my research proved to be, by far, the most comical as well as the most disgusting.

I met droves of interesting creatures and witnessed some uncommon events, such as a Yankees fan buying a drink for a Red Sox fan. Documenting animals in the wild has been incredibly easy in comparison to studying the effects of alcohol on a bipolar talking monkey. Animals tend to be semi-predictable. Humans, on the other hand, are capable of doing just about anything—especially under the influence.

The frequenters of this booze-soaked ecosystem ranged in all shapes and personalities. Some were happy and some were sad. Some were angry and others were creepy. Some were loud, some were smelly, some were aggressive, and some were just plain wild.

***

The Frequenters

This is perhaps the most important part of the book. Without the natives, the watering hole would just be a hole. Booze would spoil, timeless tunes would remain trapped in the jukebox, no joke would ever be told, and no great idea would ever be idea'd. It's the people that make the place.

In nature, native wildebeest consume grass around their drinking hole before being eaten by lions. Lions then take giant shits nearby, and eventually those piles of dung become the grass that the next generation of wildebeest will eat. In the local drinking establishment, however, bar natives release those trapped, timeless tunes from their jukebox incarceration, pass on their jokes and spread their ideas, and make damned sure that no fermented beverage spoils in vain. They ensure that the circle of life at the bar goes on.

Creatures from all walks of life congregate at the watering hole to quench their thirsts, drown their sorrows, find new partners to mate with, and to watch the big game with their chums. It's a cultural hub; an intersection of strangers bound on a collision course of different economic statuses, belief systems, sexual orientations, and liquor tastes.

Generally speaking, most bars have the same profiled visitors: The creeper, the craft beer geek, the wine snob, the lady who modifies *everything* on her food and drink order, the guy who tries to fight everyone, the loud mouth who loves to argue politics or religion, and the one or two people who have a tendency to forget to pay their tabs. There are those who make you smile from ear to ear when they pull up a barstool, and those whose arrival make you shutter with disgust. Here are some generic descriptions of commonly sighted bar regulars, as well as some of my own personal samples.

I would also like to declare that there would be no book to write if it had not been for the countless characters that I've encountered over the years of my bartending career. All of the credit is due directly to the influence—both good and bad—that these folks have had on me. Below I've included a list of the personalities—real and generic—that have shaped me as a bartender and as a person whilst behind the stick.

The Creeper

The interesting thing about a creeper is that you might not detect anything creepy about them at first. Creepers can take the form of just about anyone.

Sometimes bar guests become creepier the more you get to know them. When they become comfortable with you, they begin to lower their wall of defense. They're less apprehensive about sharing things with you. Maybe you serve them one or two more drinks than usual and then out pops an incredibly inappropriate comment or secret.

"I got into photography a little while ago as a hobby....you should totally let me take pictures of you."

"Are you walking to your car alone later?"

"Would you like to sleep with my wife while I film it?"

"Have you ever used a ball gag?"

The awkwardness catches you by surprise as you search your intellect for a way to react. Maybe whatever they said was just a Freudian slip. Maybe it was just a failed attempt at humor. Or maybe, this creepiness is at their core. It's their essence. It's what remains once all of their layers have been peeled away.

Once that boundary has been crossed, it's very hard to return to a normal and symbiotic bartender/guest relationship. Once the creeper invites you to have a threesome with his or her spouse, buys you expensive lingerie, or sends you a picture of his penis via Snap Chat, it's all over.

Wild Bill

I've learned to spot him from the parking lot as he dramatically exits his pick-up truck, and when he does, one could actually be a bit let down that he's not climbing down off of a saddled horse.

I run to the computer and queue up the theme song from *The Good, The Bad, And The Ugly*. The opening drums thunder through the speakers of the pub in perfect unison with his footsteps as he struts up to the front door. As he's greeted by the swarm of employees and other guests that adore this living legend so very much, the timeless whistle of the tune begins. I then tap the microphone head and begin to sound his official introduction that I took from Muhammad Ali, and then altered a bit.

Ladies and gentlemen...he's wrestled alligators, tussled whales, handcuffed lightning and threw thunder in jail. He murdered a rock, injured a stone, and hospitalized a brick. He's so mean he makes medicine sick! Please welcome the leanest, meanest, roughest, toughest cowboy this side of the Mississippi...Wild Bill Coreyyyyy!

As the crowd of confused guests unfamiliar to the pub and our wicked ways rubberneck around trying to figure out what the hell just happened, I am greeted at the bar by a true roughneck—an authentic throwback representative of the old wild west—a should-have-been undefeated gunslinger, victorious not for his skill with a six-shooter, but rather his charm that would have any challenger lower their weapon.

Wild Bill is a powerful and compact man, humble to his roots and unchanged by the passing years. To be honest, he seems to have stepped right out of a time-travel machine and come tramping and clinking up to a bar stool and into our lives. I say *clinking* because yes—he does on occasion wear real cowboy stirrups. It's a spectacle to see him with his son, a young buck named Layne who lives in Kentucky, when he travels north to visit his Pa'. The two strapping men, dressed to the nines in their vaquero attire, perform a wrangler waltz as they advance through the bar, scanning the room for a place to sit, eyes winced and vigilant like those of Clint Eastwood.

He's got a weathered look to him, as if he's already lived life three times over. His hands are rough and calloused from years of work and play, yet they seem to always offer the very best of handshakes. A bull riding baseball hat always hides his hair, which is surprisingly well-maintained and soft. His rounded, rosy dimples and the sprawling wrinkles at the corners of his eyes allude to a lifetime spent smiling and laughing.

At the age of 35, most men begin to take up golf or racquetball. Wild Bill took up bull riding. Again, he's not your average guy. The shrine that we have constructed behind the bar to honor the old brute includes an absolutely *EPIC* photograph of Bill riding a two-ton bucking monster off into the sunset—certainly no match for this former power lifter and concrete worker. Add to that repertoire a memorized encyclopedia of jokes, and you have a guy that would give *the most interesting man in the world* a run for his money.

Wild Bill epitomizes and embodies the true essence of a regular-turned-friend. In the bar business, we're taught to refer to customers as "guests." However, if you're lucky enough, every now and then those guests become great friends.

Mr. Wild works for PSE&G, and actually had a hand in the construction of our pub in Bordentown, New Jersey. Rightfully so, after all of that hard work, Bill decided that it was time for a beer. He was one of the very first guests to walk through the doors when we opened, and we fell in love with him instantly.

As we celebrated our first Christmas together as a watering hole, I went out and had a plaque made with the words *Wild Bill Corey* inscribed on it, and then drilled it into the bar top at his favorite barstool. We saw that he was, like most of us, a creature of habit. He always sat on the same barstool if possible, and so we wanted to honor his loyalty, generosity, and overall awesomeness with a plaque that signified that this was *his* seat.

The difference between a standard regular and Wild Bill can be seen on a busy night when the barstools are almost completely filled-up. A pair of young girls are seated in Bill's spot as he arrives a bit later than usual. A typical regular would see that their honorary seat was taken, and then throw a sarcastic yet slightly serious fit about it. Again, *not* Wild Bill.

He hovers around, greeting everyone he knows and others that he doesn't while *waiting*, not asking, to be served. Minutes and minutes will pass by leaving Wild Bill with an empty glass and still, not a peep. He just sits there, hands folded while gazing throughout the pub, politely waiting for us to get our heads out of our asses and pour him a glass of his beloved lager.

"So who's Wild Bill? And how do I get a plaque on the bar," one of the girls asks, somehow blind to the possibility that this was only the 19,748th time I've been asked that question. I loosen my belt buckle and unzip the fly of my pants.

"Well, what are you willing to do for one," I say while cracking a smile. Then I explain to them that they've already been disqualified.

"Wait, why?"

"Because you asked for it," I pointed out. I explained to them that Wild Bill has a plaque because he never asked for one.

"Well what happens if he comes in and we're sitting in his seat?"

"I don't know. How good is your health insurance?"

"No, seriously. What happens?"

"Again, I'm not sure. How about you ask him—he's sitting right next to you."

The surprised and embarrassed girls turn tomato-red, and then begin to nervously explain themselves. Before they have a chance, Bill postures up, grabs them both by the throat, and launches them out of his seat. Alas—sometimes I wish that were the case. Quite differently, however, he just smiles at them and extends his hand while introducing himself. After other seats open up, you would think that the two girls would scoot down so that he could assume his rightful place at the bar. Nope—not a chance. Brats.

"So why that seat," I asked him one day.

"It's magical," he leaned in and whispered to me during a sit-down chat I had with him, right before taking a gulp of his treasured Yuengling. "I've walked in during the day when there's only two or three people in here, and there will still be someone in that seat. Like I said, there's something special about it."

The magic of which he speaks may be that of *Cupid*—the aloof and haphazard brat of a matchmaker who seemingly fires his volleys while blindfolded and on LSD. Yet on one fateful night, he got it right and sent two arrows flying through the pub. One hit Wild Bill who had been nestled comfortably on his designated perch, and the other, a warmhearted lassie named Mary who was in town from Chicago on business.

The two caught eyes that night and fell victim to the love bug. Now, studies would show that a pub is usually not the *best* place to find true love, although it can be good hunting grounds to pick up a horny chick with daddy issues or a former high school jock, still wearing his same varsity jacket from eons ago, him boasting about the big game that took place back when he had hair and a little less herpes. But typically, a bar rarely serves as a proper venue to find your soul mate. Wild Bill and Mary, however, beat the odds and did just that.

"I was just sittin' there mindin' my own business," he recounts innocently but with a chuckle, as if he was seated in the principal's office trying to fib his way out of a detention.

"Yeah, *OK!*" Mary chimes in as she contests.

"Well, I may have winked once or twice," Bill admitted as he trailed off and took another sip, cracking a smile.

The story is that Wild Bill was seated on his barstool when he first saw Mary. After a few exchanges of smiles and head nods, Mary actually summoned *him!* Seated at a table across the room, she raised her arm into the air and made a *come hither* movement with her hand. And hither is what he did.

Now, Bill's claim to fame is his genuineness. There is absolutely nothing fraudulent or forced about him. He is who he is and that's all that he is, Dr. Seuss would say. Contrary to the vast majority of males at the watering hole, Wild Bill showed humility, chivalry, and all-around kindness during this moment of hot pursuit, and that is what Mary remembers best.

"I thought he was cute so I wanted to meet him. What I remember best about that night was his sweetness. He was a true gentleman."

See that, guys? In a bar packed-full of slobbering and peacocking alpha males trying to project their cocky "I want it but don't need it" mentality on roomfuls of apprehensive women, sometimes, a little authenticity can go a long way.

In this case, that dose of authenticity led to marriage. The two lovebirds actually took their vows *inside* the walls of the pub. Both middle-aged and without a large family to attend a ceremony, the two victims of the mythical, reckless, flying archer decided that there was no more of a fitting venue in which to say "I do" than in the place that they locked eyes for the very first time. And for that, there is a *new* plaque, resting right above the *old* plaque that reads "Mr. and Mrs. Wild Bill Corey."

They love the pub, and we love them. They visit us almost daily, and are absent only when taking romantic getaways out of town, or when having small medical procedures done, such as a triple bypass. When he went under the knife, we suggested to Bill's surgeon that he would recover much quicker if they could install a keg of Yuengling in his hospital room and pump it into him intravenously. I once even wrote a prescription note to his boss demanding that he be allowed Yuengling breaks during the workday for the sake of his health.

For me, it was truly inspiring to see a legitimate love story play out in front of my eyes, no matter how skeptical I can be of all that mushy stuff. On a busy bar night with the drinks flowing and the house band making a rumpus of things; with the chaos and strangeness of it all, I see Wild Bill, a true caballero; a real-life cowboy with his lovely lady in his arms, their eyes fixated on each other in a sort of steadfast, oblivious exchange of loving appreciation for their new soul mate that had somehow escaped them for the first fifty-something years of their lives, but of whom they bumped into on one fateful night at the pub. It's very rewarding to know that I had and still have a small part to play in such a thing.

Robin

Robin was one of my more recent regulars—my first one at the Farm and Fisherman tavern, which was the first place I worked at after getting exiled from the Irish pub.

We both struck-up conversation during one of our very first nights open as a restaurant, and we quickly bonded over the fact that we're both writers. Well, I scribe my thoughts down on paper while she is actually a paid writer. She blogs for the *Mother Nature Network* and is a very accomplished food blogger.

For me, meeting Robin was important. When I got fired from my job at the Irish pub, I thought I'd never really find an environment as intimate and closely-knit as the shire-like dwelling from which I had come. I had built an uncountable amount of friends and relationships there, and I wasn't sure that I'd encounter anything like it ever again. I was the former alpha male, now wounded and limping into a new ecosystem. I was nervous.

It didn't take long, however, for this wine and cheese fan with a strong Christian foundation to warm-up to me. We connected through discussions on food, music, and mostly—writing. It may not have seemed as such, but reeling-in my first regular at a new watering hole was a big deal for my survival as a drink slinger.

The Wine/Beer Snob

Nothing you have behind your bar will make this person happy. It's in the nature of their label of "snob." Snobs and geeks are different.

A wine or beer *geek* will ask you for some rare and would-be out of place Belgian tripel or Bordeaux just to spark conversation or debate. They already scoped out your beer or wine list and know the answer, but just want to lecture you on the brewery or vineyard tour they went on a few months back. In the end, they'll settle on almost anything you put in front of them.

A *snob*, on the other hand, will try everything on the menu that you're willing to give them a taste of, declare that it's "too big," "too light," "too oaky," "too malty," and then, with tears in their eyes, they'll say "I'll just have a club soda." It's a power thing. The snob, similarly to the geek, wants everyone to know that they're an expert. An expert perhaps, but also an asshole.

PJ

There is probably no more important regular, at least in terms of my own life, that graced my bar than PJ—a full-time firefighter, professional quad-racer, and all-around amazing guy.

The first time I talked with PJ was at an after party he threw at his house upon the culmination of the Halloween festivities that took place at the Irish pub that night. I had met him briefly during the course of the night at the bar, as it was hard not to notice the effort put into his Spartan warrior costume. That, and the fact that he drank Jägermeister and Red Bull as a cocktail. Yuck!

The party was interesting from the moment I arrived, when I saw a few cars skidding and sliding all over the front yard in the dark. I was told that PJ was really into racing, but I didn't think I'd see people drifting their sedans in the grass a few yards from the front porch.

The grounds were massive—he owns a horse farm no more than a nine-minute drive from the pub, complete with a multi-jump dirt bike track, several horse stalls, and a hot tub. And speaking of the hot tub, once inside the house, I was quickly greeted by two young women—completely bare-assed—who had just climbed out of it.

As the weeks and months passed by, I began to get to know this action-sports junkie more and more. It was usually late in the evening when he visited the pub for his Jager-Bomb-esque cocktail, and he always was great at striking-up interesting conversation with those around him. He never failed to tip extremely well, and so I started to buy him a round whenever I'd see him. But as hospitable as I thought I was being, I would quickly learn that I PJ was the real master of hospitality.

The great thing about bartending, as I mention in other parts of this book, is the capability and platform a drink slinger has to network. If you're looking for a good dentist, the odds are in your favor that someone sitting at the bar knows one, and in their buzzed and happy state, they're likely to give you the guy's personal cell number or maybe even call them on your behalf. I didn't need a dentist, but, at the time, I did need a place to live. With every passing bar shift, I mentioned it to almost everyone. Many leads and offers were sent my way, but none of them seemed intriguing. Then, PJ offered.

I moved into the *Funny Farm* (the name of his house that evolved after a slew of long nights and confusing mornings) not long after. When PJ's not fighting fires, you can often find him running shows at *Monster Jam* or competing in races all over the country and world. Because of this, he's not home much. He brought my friend Vince and myself on board to replace those who had moved-out, and to look after the place while he was out gallivanting. The house was monstrous, the area gorgeous, the garages filled with motored toys, the rent very reasonable, and his policies forgiving when I hit a tough patch. I was lucky to be taken in by such a generous person.

To give thanks to this legendary landlord, I aimed to bring the fun as much as possible. And so I did. The farm quickly became the place to be after 2am. We hosted lots of friends and strangers alike; the young and the old, as well as the scared and the brave. I quickly learned that, at a ripe forty-something years old, PJ could out-party just about everyone. He was usually the last one to pass out and the first one to get up in the morning—and that's including all of the girls who came over and had been shamed in one form or another the night prior and whom were trying to make a quick, early-morning escape to save their dignity. The house was living up to its nickname shortly after I moved in. It became home to me, and I owe the shelter I enjoyed for several years of my life to the man, the myth, the legend—PJ.

Meg

Meg is, like most of my favorite people, an intelligent, deep thinker. It's funny that we became friends on a night that could've easily ended with me throwing her out of the pub, actually. Whenever Meg, her sister Kate, and another friend of theirs named John would arrive, I knew that I was in for a fun night. They had no problem being my guinea pigs for any strange concoctions that I was conjuring-up behind the bar —well, they had no problem drinking just about anything I gave them.

Per usual, after about ten shots or so, the napkins began to be shredded, coasters would be thrown in every direction, french fries would be littered all over the floor, and the bar top would be covered in ketchup and sticky liquor. But instead of scolding Meg and her merry band of marauders for their delinquency, I celebrated them. They always arrived to have a good time, and because of that, everyone else around them would have a good time as well—especially me.

72

Meg was actually involved in a flash rave that broke out at the Irish pub one night. It was a slow and boring evening, and so we decided to switch gears a bit. Shit ended up getting weird, and there's only a few of us who remain to speak of it. That's what happens when Meg gets bored—she starts raves.

A fellow travel addict and fan of good beer, she often frequented my bar during the later hours of the evening to talk, listen, laugh, and cry. Upon arrival, she'd greet me at the bar with an enormous sigh and visual desperation for a drink after a long week of thesis writing. Once she vented about whatever she needed to vent about, she was ready to let loose and have a great time. She got along with just about anyone and often played musical chairs as she floated around the room like the social butterfly she is. Similarly to many of my other regulars, Meg became a trusted friend of mine over the years. She's got the travel bug in the same way I do, and is someone who sees her home neither here nor there.

Brian

Brian was one of the nicest regulars I've ever met who had almost *nothing* nice to say—ever. He drives limousines for a living and usually visited me during the evening hours. An amateur comedian with a dry and sarcastic sense of humor, Brian would always find something to complain or make fun of me about. At first, he was like an annoying gnat that I couldn't swat away. But after time, I began to get used to him—like the wart on my big toe.

Because of the upscale and uptight environment that he worked in, he would come to our pub late at night craving arguments and dirty jokes. His political correctness meter was maxed-out while driving ritzy people around the tri-state area during the day, and so when he sat his ass onto one of our barstools, he would unleash his hounds over a Dogfish Head 90-Minute IPA and a plate of chicken fingers. It didn't take too long for me to "get" him, though. Once I realized that it was crudeness that he craved, I hit whatever verbal curveball he threw at me right back between his eyes. We'd insult each other's taste in clothing, movies, beer—even each other's mothers—all in the company of other bar guests. They always looked at us like we were crazy.

Once we both had enough, he'd pay his tab and say goodbye while trying to hold back a smile, a feat that became harder and harder for him to accomplish.

Jay and Tiff

These guys flat out suck! I've never met such a repulsive, annoying, cheap, and smelly couple in my entire life. They were the bane of my bartending existence; the coyote to my roadrunner; the Steve Urkel to my Carl Winslow. I wish a plague of skunks and homeless beggars upon their household.

When Jay and Tiff began to frequent the Irish pub, I immediately began to cut myself to release the angst that their scratchy laughter instilled in me. At one point, I was considering going on Craigslist to find an assassin who'd whack them both so that I wouldn't have to see their goofy faces ever again. But when I realized that Craigslist is designed for pedophiles and not necessarily good freelance hit men, I decided to take matters into my own hands.

They thought that I was serving them beers with kindness, when in all reality, I was picking my nose and offloading gigantic, gummy bear-sized boogers into their beverages. I'd smile at them when they told me whatever stupid story that I couldn't care less about, and as soon as they turned away for even a second, I gave them the bird and threw karate kicks at their head, missing by mere millimeters.

Sike! These guys were some of the very best friends I've made at any one of my watering holes. I'm just still incredibly jealous that Jay beat me in my family's ugly sweater Christmas contest last year. Asshole. But seriously, if you're reading this (and you better fucking be reading this) I love you both. I just wanted to break-up the mush-fest a bit, and you were the lucky winners.

Lou and Rose

In their long and drawn-out search for a proper watering hole to hang out at on a Friday after yet another grinding week of work, they stumbled into the Irish pub, pulled-up a pair of barstools, and sat down for a drink. Do I remember this occasion? No, absolutely not. Do I remember the first time I had a conversation with this married couple of 25 years? No, I don't. But after talking with them and hearing about why they began to frequent our pub instead of the many others close by, I couldn't help but feel good about what I do for a living—and how well it seemed I was doing it.

There was no special treatment. "We came into the pub and you, Danny, Art—you all seemed to give a shit, for lack of better words."

Despite Rose's strong ties to Christianity, she has quite the potty mouth at times.

"At every place we've gone to before, we always felt like just a another customer. We would walk in, sit down, have a few drinks and a bite to eat, and then leave. We never really felt a connection."

I was enjoying this little trip into the past as we tried to trace how exactly we became so close.

"You made us laugh and that was it! To be honest, I don't remember the service. The food could have sucked. The beer could have stunk or had flies in it—whatever—it didn't matter to us. What mattered was that you were genuinely interested in us. We had fun, and that's why we came back."

They came back, alright. Lou and Rose spent approximately $300 per month during a span of over four years at a pub that's prices are fairly reasonable. Over time, their patronage became habitual—for them and for us—and if there ever passed a Friday evening when they *weren't* spotted, people began to mutter and worry. The following night or week when I'd see them next, I'd scold them like an angry father for not informing me of their whereabouts and for breaking routine. "You can't do that to me, guys! I'm too young to get wrinkles!"

That $300 per month figure is not a typo. And they're not wealthy aristocrats either. Their middle-class income allows for a humble yet comfortable lifestyle in their one-floor rancher with their two cars, two chihuahuas, and Lou's pride and joy—a 60-something-inch flat screen tube to watch *The Walking Dead, Game of Thrones,* and the Oakland Raiders on. They spend their week like most normal hardworking

Americans—reporting to and clocking-out of a job that they're not too fond of. They work and live for the weekend.

The process of making a home at our pub was a subtle one. First, it was a basic introduction and good bar service. Next, it was memorized drinks, handshakes, and bullshitting. Then it was placing their drinks on the bar surface before they had a chance to sit down, followed by customized food orders and extra goodies from the kitchen. Soon after, we began to notice that they tipped *really* well. I'm talkin' 50-100% gratuity at times. That's right; if their bill ended up being $50, it was normal to receive from them a tip that was anywhere between $25-$50! Who other than someone who works for the mob, or *pretends* to work for the mob, does that?!

After about seven years behind the stick, I still feel semi-guilty when someone leaves a large tip that I feel I didn't really deserve. With Lou and Rose, I often felt like a whore or a conman robbing honest, hardworking folk of their retirement money. I mean, people tip 15-20% because that's what's expected in our restaurant culture in this present day and age. That's the norm. Any less than that, and you're going to get the stink-eye from your bartender or server. Leave more than that as a tip, and it feels like you're paying me to be your friend—kind of weird.

Before long, I started to understand why Lou and Rose treated us so well. With the likes of Danny, Art (both of whom you'll read more about in the coming pages), and myself behind the bar constantly smashing plates of whipped cream in each others' faces, talking shit about sports, scotch-taping paper tags with extremely inappropriate words and phrases on each others' backs, and even wrestling, they had no need to travel to the nearest comedy club to get their laughs—they had found one just a few blocks away from home.

"Ya know, kid, we went to bars all over the place and it was the same thing—a drink, some food, and then the check. We never really felt a connection to anyone. We never felt special. I know that sounds corny, but you guys made us feel special since day one," Lou admitted to me over dinner and drinks not too long ago.

"We work all week at our shitty jobs dealing with our shitty bosses counting down the days until we're back into the pub on Friday for happy hour. You guys give us something to look forward to. The closer we get to Friday—man! It's like seeing the light at the end of the tunnel. And when we get to the pub and are greeted by so many of you guys, it just makes us feel great. For those few hours that we're there, we forget about how much we hate our jobs. You guys have no idea how much Rose and I depend on stories of your guys' nights out, your pranks, or even your dick jokes."

I have a very vivid memory of him looking up as if to collect himself and break-up the momentum of this uncharacteristically intimate disclosure. He took a sip of his beer, smiled, and then continued.

"When we walk into the pub, we're on vacation. It lasts for a few hours, and then we're good to go. After a night with all of you guys, all of our stress disappears and we're recharged for Monday morning. That, to us, is worth *way* more than what we spend at the pub each month."

Jesus, Lou! I can't handle this pressure! I mean, we're just bartenders, right? Many of us are just passing through, trying to pay our way through school or out of a gambling debt. And furthermore, you guys are just guests! Customers! Patrons! You're just people that pay me money—a lot of money—to pour you some beer, serve you some food, and entertain you a bit. ¿Verdad? No. Falso.

When Lou and Rose walk into the pub, they are bombarded with hugs and kisses from the hostess, the servers, the bartenders, managers, and loads of other guests. Even the infamous Chef Jay waddles out from the kitchen in his pajama pants and freshly-stained apron to greet this wonderful couple as he shares his daily specials with them. Lou and Rose are not guests, nor customers, nor patrons. And it's safe to say that they don't view us simply as bartenders or servers either. At this point, even if they simply stopped tipping altogether, I would tend to them in the same manner that I do now—as if they're family. They did, after all, unofficially adopt me.

When my real parents finally met Lou and Rose, it was reminiscent of the "bizarro world" episode of *Seinfeld*, in which Elaine begins to spend time with three guys that eerily resemble Jerry, George, and Kramer. Eventually, Elaine finds herself standing between the two groups of mirrored men in an awkward standoff, trying to choose the right company for the evening.

As she begins to walk away with her new friends, Jason Alexander's character steps forward and bashfully asks if he could join. Elaine turns him down and says "sorry, but... we've already got a George." It was a similar standoff when my two sets of parents stared each other down for the first time, one pair tugging at my left arm and the other pulling on my right. Kidding, actually. They both get along perfectly as expected.

So a few paragraphs ago, I began to discuss the evolution of our relationship with Lou and Rose. After the memorized drinks, the handshakes, and the bullshitting, came the hugs, kisses on the cheek, and holiday gifts. Then it was birthday celebrations. Soon after, we were being invited to each other's houses for parties and dinners. Just as they've admitted that we've been there for them, they've been there for us in the same light. And as a testament to that, my fellow bartender Kathleen has since moved into their house as they not just offered, but *insisted* that she do so—rent free—to help her with the costs of college as she works her way through school by slinging drinks. What's their reason for such generosity?

"Because you guys mean the world to us and we miss having young people around running amuck," Rose says.

Not even Muhammad Ali could have predicted the impact that we would have on each other's lives once they came walking through the front doors of the pub. This is the magic of the watering hole exemplified. This is it. This is what it's all about. It's where strangers become the best of friends. It's where those friends then become a tribe—and the tribe looks out for each other.

Customers first, then guests, then friends, and now family. Nowadays, I'm often watching sports or *The Walking Dead* on Lou's television in the company of both Lou and Rose, their new roommate Kathleen, their extremely overweight house cat Sonny, and their two cracked-out Chihuahuas, Reeba and Raider. I couldn't help but laugh when, after eating a dinner that Kathleen recently prepared for everyone, Lou gathered the empty plates and glasses en route to the kitchen sink.

"Oh, how the tables have turned," I said with a smirk. "Feels nice to be on this side of the bar for once."

The Modifier

"Can I have a Cosmo? But instead of vodka, can you use gin? And instead of triple sec or Cointreau, I want you to squeeze 1 ¼ orange wedges into it. And I only want three dashes of lime—make sure it's exactly three. And I don't want cranberry. Now, I want that stirred, not shaken, and I want only half of the dirty rocks as well."

Once you finally get the drink right to her liking after six tries, she's ready to order some grub. "How's the salmon," she asks.

How the fuck do you expect me to answer that question?! 'It's horrible, but I think you should cram it down your throat anyway?'

"OK, well I'll take the salmon, but I don't want the skin. And instead of an entire filet, can I just order half and then get a few shrimp instead? But I don't want the shrimp to be chewy. Also, I want rice pilaf but without the pilaf, and can they eliminate the seasonal vegetables and throw some fries on there instead? But with the fries, I want them tossed with some rosemary, but not too much rosemary, OK? I don't like a lot of rosemary."

81

After spending twenty minutes of your life at the P.O.S. system sending her *Iliad* of an order through to the kitchen, the plate finally comes out and she starts chomping away.

"Excuse me! Excuuuse meee! Bartender!"

I can only stave off her incessant cackling for so long. As I turn away from the guest that I am currently serving to give her the death glare, I see her holding her arms up in the air like a soccer player calling for a foul.

"These fries have too much rosemary on them. I told you that I only wanted them tossed with a *little* rosemary."

"I'm sorry ma'am, I can have the kitchen make you some new fries. They'll be right out."

"Don't bother. I'm not even that hungry, anyway." It's right after you see her barely-touched plate pushed towards the edge of the bar covered with her dinner napkin that you begin to brainstorm ways to kill her.

The Sicilian

The Sicilian is an old soul keen to the petite and occult phenomenon that life presents to us all, but goes unnoticed by most.

A top bookkeeper for a *Fortune 500* company, this marathon runner and admirer of the Mediterranean lifestyle first found his way onto one of my barstools simply out of the convenience of proximity, as he lived with his wife and two boys in a house not too far away from the Italian joint I worked at. And as much as his affluent look suits the style of the area, I noticed that he behaved like an outsider. Anyone who peered closer, beyond his well-tailored shirts, classy

Italian shoes, and glimmering wristwatch, would notice that he often left us. For a few seconds at a time, he escaped his present state and arrived on the shores of Sicily or the vineyards of the Rioja region of Spain. It is where he belongs.

He was always alone during happy hour, leaned back and loose in his posture with one arm rested on the bar holding his glass. He'd sit there sipping his Kettle One vodka on the rocks with a lime wedge, staring off into space, contemplating the ins and outs of life on this flying, organic rock we call Earth.

I'd always ask him about his day at work. With a smile and an elaborate sigh, he would typically respond with a positive, assuring adage of sorts—nothing snobbish or too polished, but instead, a comment that was quick and meaningful. It was a brief word or phrase that would crack a smile on your face shortly after walking away to pour another patron's drink. "This is all we have—this moment," he would often say in his subtle New York accent. "The rest is bullshit."

When I first met him, I kept thinking that he was an assassin or some kind of thumb bender-backer employed by the mob. But when I really got to know him, I realized that he didn't have a mean bone in his body. I mean, the guy is a mesomorph—an athletic freak—who, well into his 40s, recently joined the 100,000 mile club for distance run over a lifetime. If you ran your mouth to him, he wouldn't have minded bending your thumb back until you cried out uncle. But generally, he was more interested in discussing Van Gogh's *The Starry Night* rather than making someone see stars with his fists.

For me, bartending was the initial catalyst that sparked our friendship. It was the rope bridge that connected our very different worlds and economic stratification. When he would pull-up a barstool and sip on the drink I made for him, our perceptions would collide. He would share his wisdom and I would crack a joke or two and make him laugh after a long day of crunching numbers.

I've learned a lot from him. We discussed what mattered and what didn't, what's bullshit and what's not. As the guys to his left argued about whether or not Tom Brady was better than Peyton and the girls to his right compared Instagram shots, the Sicilian and I would debate fate versus free will, Italian versus Spanish wine, flamenco versus jazz, or *Braveheart* versus *Gladiator*—heavy talk for a neighborhood grill or pub. But most of all, we would both try to figure out, of all the geographical patches the Earth has to offer, what the fuck we were doing in central New Jersey. It's a big world, yet our adventurous spirits were rooted there, and we were always puzzled as to how that came to be.

We were two displaced souls longing to be somewhere else, and after just a few cocktails, his eyes would water when he softly spoke of his beloved shores of the Mediterranean Sea. "When I die, I want to be in Sicily, sitting in my rocking chair with a glass of red wine in my hand, looking out at the sea." Of anyone I've ever met in my entire life that has said anything about how they want to go out, I know that he will be the one to have it end as such.

Deloris

She enters the bar slowly, but not cautiously. She's been to this watering hole many, many times before. As she struts her jiggling self through the entrance and past the cocktail tables, she stalks her spot at the bar, all while winking at smiling at people that, sadly for her, are not actually paying attention.

She scopes out the scene, scanning the crowd for familiar faces and potential mates. She then pulls back a barstool, strips down to her zebra-striped top, and sits down. She's ready to tongue- kiss her glass of cheap Merlot and visually rape the young stud behind the bar who's servin' 'em up. It's Friday night, and Deloris is on the hunt.

Who or what is Deloris? The name *Deloris* is code speak for the great evil that terrorizes bars across the land in female form: a goblin or pixie whom with her inappropriate behavior and schizophrenic tendencies haunts bartenders and leaves their guests feeling disturbed and violated.

She's often a self-nominated local celebrity who's permanently stuck in her glory years of the past. A Deloris can have a variety of employment and financial backgrounds. Sometimes she's a career diner waitress who spends her hard-earned money on cigarettes and perms. In other cases, she was an unknown shadow while growing up, whom with grit and determination fueled by resentment and anger, propelled her way through college and up the corporate ladder so that she could eventually shit on all of those who never paid her much attention. Either way, she's loud, obnoxious, abrasive, offensive, egotistical, delusional, and man is she HORNY!

This special breed never leaves the hut without playing "paint by numbers" on her face, smearing enough makeup on her mug that would make the band mates of Kiss tilt their heads in wonder like confused puppies. Her radioactive lipstick burns half-moon shaped, permanent blemishes into the rim of her glass. And the stench! Her undeniably noticeable mix of cheap perfume and cigarettes, which if at all visible would look like the cloud of dirt that surrounds and follows Pigpen in *Charlie Brown,* proceeds to clog the windpipes of the masses, immediately resulting in rashing on exposed skin, singeing of nose hairs, and a sensation of confusion and disgust amongst those nearby. She eventually succeeds in gaining the attention of the other guests at the watering hole. She relishes in it.

The hair—oh the horror! Deloris' "do" is best described as a floppy afro of black, curly pubes. A bush—unkempt for a lifetime—sprouts from the cusp of her head where it grows without restriction. This baby would snag the teeth of a diesel-powered hedge trimmer. In fact, her mad nest of squiggly strands would probably serve as the safest of havens for most small woodland creatures. Beyond her wearing the occasional low-cut blouse, my eyes are thankful to never have gotten a glimpse of her chest or back, both of which I'm sure are quite furry and carpet-like.

After a long night, there tends to be a lot of chatter amongst the bartenders about what we imagine Deloris' vagina looks like, or worse—what it might *smell* like. "Do you think it talks," one of my fellow bartenders, Laff, once questioned. The reaction was priceless, in that our laughter simultaneously transformed into a shivering disgust.

The created image of Deloris' disastrous downtown is often the subject of many "would you rather" scenarios. I picture it to look something like the head of the alien that Will Smith knocked out in the movie *Independence Day*. You know, the part when the beast is laying lifeless on the table as the scientist (who looks like Fabio of the Crypt) begins to dissect it, when all of a sudden...*WHAM!* It violently snaps open, exposing its oozing, stinking membrane as all of the grown men in the room instantly take cover. "Jesus, Deloris! Close your legs!"

"It smelled like slow death in there...malaria...this was the end of the river, alright," Martin Sheen's character in *Apocalypse Now* muttered, describing Kurtz' hidden layer. Speculatively, a similar description might be used to portray Deloris' snatch—a portal to Hades, lined with hundreds of small, razor-sharp piranha teeth, slightly curved inwards so that the immediate dismembering of the dong would occur upon extraction. Nibblets of corn that fell off of the cob and down her bathing suit lay lodged in her thorn bush of afro-pube vaginal hair for all of eternity.

While sober, Deloris is actually not all that unbearable. She usually visits with a funny remark about the day; something pertaining to a thought she had while on the toilet or maybe something about an episode of Jerry Springer. She's usually somewhat friendly shortly after arriving, and on rare occasion, a pleasant guest to have seated at your bar...*gulp*... I can't believe I just admitted that.

Something changes, however, after Deloris has that first glass or two of cheap wine or scotch. It seems that "El duende" climbs out of her subconscious. It begins with slight peacocking and heckling at us behind the bar.

"Your tie has a stain on it," she squawks. "You're hair looks ridiculous!"

"Oh really," I inquire. "And yours looks nice and well-managed. What kind of conditioner do you use?"

After another glass of cheap house wine or a scotch and water, her eyes glaze over. I sense a great barbarity approaching.

She begins to glare with an irrefutable disdain as an "I hate you but I don't know why" look burns in her eyes. Another drink and the transformation is complete. Whatever decency that was keeping its head above the Merlot in her gut has now drowned in vain.

As if a nearby mad scientist pulls the lever of his Deloris-stein machine, she instantaneously turns into a monster. I can feel her eyes raping me from across the room as I wash dirty glasses or make drinks for other guests. I glance back at her and theatrically shake my head in disapproval, but it has no effect. She slithers her tongue between her buck teeth and through her half-open mouth, slowly and deliberately sliding it from side to side, telegraphing her desire to blow me. This all takes place in front of guests young and old, friends and strangers. I don't like it.

On one extra lonely and frustrating night for Deloris, she seemed a bit more ornery than usual. I could tell that she wasn't herself. There was no peacocking, no inappropriately bad jokes or behavior—not even any tongue gymnastics. The strange part was that I actually felt out of my element. I was the ying without my yang. To me, her disgusting behavior is familiar and expected. She's always been my project or maybe even my challenge, in a sense. But not on this night. It was like having an ass wart removed. You're better off without it, but it's weird at first—especially after all of that time feeling like you're sitting on a skittle.

While sitting in silence and disconnection, she continued to put down glass after glass of her truth serum. Finally, London Bridge came a' topplin' down.

"What?!" she barked at me like an angry, starving coyote, paranoid of losing its fresh kill.

"What do you mean, 'what?'" I responded a bit off-guard.

"You haven't said *one* thing to me all night! I've been waiting for you to talk to me," she growled as a bubble of saliva leaped off of her lip and onto the bar top. "I've been sitting here this whole time and you just avoid me like I'm a bother."

Hmm. Go figure.

"That's ridiculous," I yelled as I defended myself. "We're busy and I'm by myself back here. I've been running around for hours now. I'm sorry that I don't have an abundance of time for your heckling tonight."

"Yeah, but you have plenty of time to flirt with those tramps at the other end of the bar."

She was referring to two very nice, very attractive women in their thirties who were seated at the bar as well. I admittedly had spent a little extra time with them when I found out that they were exotic dancers. Our pub wasn't necessarily a normal hangout for strippers (excluding, of course, the many occasions that I've shown my bare ass to roomfuls of people), so naturally I was intrigued. When a dolphin swims up your local river, you instinctively give heed to it. I'm a guy, and I'm attracted to boobs. So what?

"Ahhh enough out of you," I said jokingly, trying to ease the tension. I puckered my lips, clenched my fists, and swallowed every bit of pride that I could. "You know you're my...*gulp*...number one, darling!"

"Yeah, yeah, yeah," she snapped back in a true New Jerseyan tone. "Whatevah."

Something incredible happened next: She put her head down, her eyes completely fixated on her almost empty glass of wine. I saw real human emotion in her face. The fight in her momentarily slipped away. I saw tears welling up in her eyes. I felt horrible—an unfamiliar sadness in the pit of my stomach. Her guard was dropping.

I didn't know what to do or say, so I retreated and got the hell out of dodge. I walked over to the two strippers who immediately asked me what was going on with Deloris, who at the time was seated all by her lonesome with her head in her hands. I reassured them that she was fine, and that this was normal behavior. The concerned women, however, didn't buy it.

One of them, tall and blonde with crystal-blue eyes and an absolutely beautiful floral tattoo sleeve—almost amazon-like in her appearance—walked over to Deloris and asked if she would like to join them at the other side of the bar for a drink. After being turned down, the woman gently placed her hands on Deloris' shoulders in a comforting manner, reassuring her that she was welcome to join if she changed her mind.

I thought it was a very nice gesture, and a welcome one at that, being that the attention was off of me for a second. But my peace was short-lived.

"How *dare* you," she snarled, her mascara trickling down her face inside the water bubbles of a few tears.

"Excuse me?," I inquired, surprised and a bit startled.

"I don't need your pity *OR* theirs!" She followed that with a barrage of cursing and insults—showering me in wine-stained saliva as she spat her message of disapproval.

"Look, I don't know what you're talking about. All that I said to the ladies was that you were enjoying your peace and quiet. I didn't ask them to invite you to have a drink with them. Did it ever occur to you that there are nice, courteous people out there who might just be interested in having a good time with others? They just wanted you to join them. What's the problem with that?"

"Why would *anyone* want my company? No one wants me!"

Here we go, I thought.

As a bartender, it's always my strategy to disrupt any uncomfortable moment with humor. I'm certainly not a comedian, but I try.

"There's 6 billion people on this earth Deloris! There's gotta be someone."

"Look at me! I'm old, fat, and lonely!"

"Well at least you have nice hair," I joked once more. I walked away to serve another drink and could see that she was not laughing with me. She began to sob, taking deep breaths in between words and phrases while she wiped dripping snot on her sleeve. I gave her a napkin.

"It's over. I'm tired of going home alone every night. I feel so alone all of the time, and...the worst part..." she paused to blow her honker. (It's funny how all conversation and background noise often seems to come to an abrupt halt right before someone says something extremely awkward or inappropriate, which is then heard by the entire room. This occasion was no different.)

"I haven't gotten laid in *YEARS*," she cried out. You could hear a cocktail cherry stem drop and hit the floor at that point.

Everyone's eyes in the bar leaped onto us, then back to their drinks, friends, or the televisions, followed shortly by smirks and giggles, their hands covering their lips as they all mouthed the words *oh my God!* I put my head down.

After her embarrassing outburst, she looked into my eyes and asked me for another drink. I refused. I told her I couldn't serve her anymore, and after she argued for a brief moment, she understood why.

"Well can I please have a glass of water," she pleaded like Oliver Twist. I obliged. I placed the water in front of her and just stood there. I knew she wanted to talk more.

"Why doesn't anyone want me, Jay? I just don't want to be lonely anymore."

I took a deep breath and then exhaled slowly. Deloris, as awful of a heckler as she may be, is a decent person deep down, really not much different than anyone else who struggles with bouts of loneliness. I gave her my opinion; brutal and honest. I told her that she will never find anyone if she continues to enjoy being the villain, the heckler of the room. It's a transparent psychological phenomenon—the act of closing people off to avoid being hurt in the long run. I told her that I believed that this is what she was doing.

I continued to divulge to her, quite mercilessly, how bartenders that deal with her bullshit on a daily or weekly basis feel about her antics and her attitude. I told her what other people say and whisper about her once she leaves or as they see her walking into the bar.

Her jaw dropped and she began to well-up again.

I felt like I did what needed to be done. I scolded her. I made her aware of the flaws that most people see in her—flaws that are completely forced and unnatural. I made the claim that she drives people away purposefully as a defense mechanism.

"You'll never find love if you continue to close people off, Deloris. I've sat here and watched you turn guys down one after the other—*real winners*," I enunciated sarcastically as I tried to get her to crack a smile. "Those guys wanted to buy you a drink of your beloved house scotch, but you scoffed at them and shooed them off like barflies. Well, what makes you think that the same isn't likely to continue to happen to you?"

"You still haven't answered my question," she reminded me. "Why would anyone want to be with me?"

"Deloris, if I didn't care about you, I would not be sitting here psychoanalyzing you. You have friends here whether you think it or not, even though the first thing you do when you sit down is bark for your drink and insult or heckle us. We put up with your shit on a daily basis because you're part of the family here—maybe the estranged and crazy aunt—but family regardless."

I went on scolding her for her own good. I made her aware of all of her shenanigans that we consider annoying and offensive, which include her incessant complaining, nagging, and sloppiness after a few drinks.

"You're just a bartender. What do you know," she interrupted.

Less offended as I should have been after that remark, I tried to jam through her waxy ears and into her thick skull the concept or idea that the people who serve your drinks can be much more observant than one would think. We interact with people on a very informal level before, during, and after the ingestion of alcohol—the truth juice.

Most bartenders are cognizant of minor details that go overlooked by most, including miniscule physical mannerisms, nervous ticks, the condition of a wedding ring, the timing of changes in behavior in relation to drinks consumed, or the size of someone's pupils. Our livelihood depends on attention to detail.

"You're right, Deloris. I'm just a bartender. I don't have a psychology degree, but this (as i began to waive my arms around the bar) is my life. This is my schoolhouse education. We see and deal with more than you could wrap around that luscious head of hair of yours. Let me ask you something, Deloris. Why is it that you would rather come and sit at my bar and spend three or four times as much money on cheap booze when you could easily buy it at the liquor store and drink it at home?"

I told her that I had to go serve another guest, and that I'd be back to hear her answer.

When I returned, she obliged. "Because I'm lonely at home. Because you guys always have a way of cheering me up and making me laugh. Because I go through my workday being fake, and dealing with fake people, but when I come here, I can just let go."

"Letting go is an understatement, love," I said as I smirked.

"You come here to be in the company of others, but you constantly try to drive people away. I've seen you be very charming and funny—an absolute delight. And your jokes! Your jokes are as dirty and tasteless as anyone's and they always make us laugh. You need to put the claws away and stop being afraid of letting people get close to you. If not, you will continue to go home alone every night."

Upon the culmination of my lecture, I saw an emerging look of acceptance—maybe even epiphany in her eyes. Perhaps my words had broken through her cloud of perfume and planted a seed in her brain.

"So no psychology degree, huh?" she questioned as she winked, expectedly nanoseconds from slithering her tongue between her teeth once more. Yet she didn't. She held back. She just smiled and asked for her check.

I had hoped that she learned something that night. I hoped that I had played a part in a moment of enlightenment for her. She was one of the last guests to leave that night, and when she finally buggered off, I began my closing duties at the pub. As tiresome and mundane as these procedures are, they offer me a time to reflect on the night and a chance to take a breath, loosen up my tie, and relax a bit. It's often a time of great clarity. I felt really good about myself and my job.

As I walked into work the following night, ready for yet another exciting and behaviorally revealing experience at the watering hole, I wondered if anything that I had said to Deloris had seeped through her pube-afro and into her brain. I was eventually joined at the bar by a new couple whom I hadn't met before, both in their 40s, on a slower-than-average night. It was only them and a few scattered folks enjoying some Guinness and shepherd's pie, when in walked you know who.

I was actually surprisingly pleased to see her, and was excited to discuss her breakthrough revelations on how she'd taken into account all of my words and advice from her prior visit. It was a modest hope.

"Where is everyone?! This place is *dead*," she squawked in her all-to-familiar squawk.

"Hi, Deloris," I said as I clenched my teeth, eyes wide in an attempt to send her a nonverbal message to behave herself. Out of courtesy, I introduced her to the innocent and adorable couple who were about to enjoy their last moments of peace and quiet that night. Typical of Deloris, she showed no interest in them, and shrugged them off rudely.

"So, about last night," she started. "If you want me so much, why don't you just take me to pound town in the bathroom right now? I wore my special thong for youuu."

I shivered with the willies, smiled embarrassingly at the violated and disturbed couple, and once again placed a coaster in front of our beloved heckling wench.

"Welcome back, Deloris."

6

The Bartenders

As a seasoned zoologist, I share several traits with the bartenders in this study. For instance, I typically work during the nocturnal hours being that, in the wild, the most shocking animal behavior usually takes place in that time slot. It's fairly boring to me to watch a pride of lions interact with each other during the day, being that they just lay there and scratch themselves.

Comparably, from what I observed at the bipedal watering hole, most of the shocking, dramatic events crazy occurred during some of those same nocturnal hours. I met, sniffed, and then interacted with several interesting frequenters during the daytime, but in no way, shape, or form did it compete with the yelling, dancing, fighting, vomiting, or mating calls that the dark hours entailed. The period of time that is referred to as 'last call' is quite possibly the most captivating span of twenty minutes that can be observed on Earth. It is, in all essence, the last-ditch effort of the evening for those at the watering hole to poison themselves.

These bartenders seemed to always have the attention of the rest of the gatherers at the local bar ecosystem. They were often the loudest and the liveliest, and they usually established some sort of alpha status or understanding of hierarchy with the others in the room. It seemed to be in the best interest for the entire population. I especially relate to this custom because of my own job descriptions. If I am cornered by a predator or even by a defensive mother who's trying to protect her young, it is imperative that I establish my dominance. If I don't, it's game over.

I think the strongest bond that bartenders and I share, however, exists in the fact that, while working either in the wild or at the local pub, we're often surrounded by hoards of unpredictable and entertaining creatures. Sometimes, while swimming through caves or climbing up to the canopy of the jungle, I see things that make me laugh, cry, shutter, and philosophize. After discussing the life and job of a bartender with those in this study, it's easy to draw lines that connect our two exciting and strange professions.

***

Now that you've met some of the kind, hilarious, outlandish, and gross folks that frequent the local watering hole, it's time to meet those acting zookeepers who pour poison into a glass, give it to a guest, and receive money in return.

Some choose this kind of lifestyle while others get sucked into it like a drug addiction. In fact, many get sucked into bartending *because* of a drug addiction. But no matter the size, shape, color, orientation, amount of tats and piercings, education level, or number of misdemeanors, bartenders are some of the most interesting, deranged, hilarious, impulsive, and innovative people that walk the face of the Earth.

Below is a list—a small one at that—which describes and pays homage to my brothers and sisters-in-arms. I've pulled back-to-back-to-back doubles with these guys, gotten wasted and thrown up along side them, and laughed and cried with them. Most of all, however, I've learned from and been inspired by them.

What I've written about these people, for the most part, correlates directly to the foundation of this book and what I have been hoping to achieve by it—providing an honest and analytical look into the ecosystem of the proverbial local watering hole. These are the folks at the core of it all.

Danny

In his personal photo album lies a still shot of Danny launching his high school diploma into the abyss of the Grand Canyon in the form of a meticulously constructed paper airplane—an image that best portrays his creativity and extremism for the unorthodox.

A child plagued with ailments that left him fighting an uphill battle to survive, bed-ridden for most of his early childhood, Danny has spent the rest of his life trying to make up for lost time, morphing into a glutton for all things fun. He's got an appreciation for life and good people that is all too rare in this world. And although his heart may have been in a weakened state while growing up, it has evolved into solid gold.

The guy's a real picaroon—an absolute savage in his search for adventure and sensory-stimulating conquests. He's one of those dudes that immediately raises the performance bar once he enters a room—you either become sharper, wittier, and more dynamic, or be left in the dust. A seeker of good company, food, and drink, at 160 lbs soaking wet, he gulps down his beloved Magner's Irish cider like a blue whale inhaling tons of gallons of ocean water before filtering it for plankton.

His life stories sound fantastical, even imaginary at times with the amount of bizarre details and events that encircle these tales of pillage and plunder, until, of course, someone speaks up and vouches for him seemingly out of nowhere. I owe much to him in terms of my employment and survival as a bartender, but even more in terms of his friendship. He is the grandmaster, and I, the young grasshopper.

One thing I quickly learned about Danny was not to cross him. He is a diabolical, cerebral, and well-oiled revenge machine. He once told me a story of an incident that took place while he and his monster brothers—complete genetic opposites—were sailing the high seas on a quest to land the big kahuna. They had chartered a private fishing vessel for the evening, and after hours of catching nothing but boots, tires, and small bait fish, they returned to port with almost empty hands and sky-high BAC levels.

Before disembarking the vessel, however, Danny wanted to have a word with the captain. He noticed during the trip that instead of actively seeking new fishing spots with higher activity on the fish finder, the skipper of this particular boat spent most of the time cuddling with his girlfriend on the bridge instead. Danny staggered drunkenly up to him, chewed him out for neglecting his duties, raised his right arm, and smacked the guy across the face with a fish!

The captain of a vessel—a historically sacred figure—being assaulted on his own grounds by a drunk, skinny guy armed with a limp, slimy, stinking striper. The audacity! Throughout history, a crime of this degree was (and in some areas of the world still is) punishable by death. If a bitter sailor had ever taken a codfish to Captain Cook's cabeza, he would have been shuffled off the plank with great haste. But that's Danny—tap dancing on the line of limitation, completely fearless as he walloped this underachieving angler. To me, coming home with that story makes up for the money they lost on their unsuccessful voyage that night.

On a separate occasion, not too long ago, Danny found himself in a feces throwing contest with a local car dealership after purchasing a Jeep that began to fall apart shortly after driving it off of the lot. Again, unless you're the joker, your odds of outsmarting Danny are not on your side. And the odds of you beating him in a game of "chicken" are all but non-existent. He will always go that extra mile to make sure that he comes out on top.

After weeks and weeks of inquiring about taking the dealership up on guaranteed offers to refurbish and repair his clunker, he finally became fed up with all of the empty promises and unreturned phone calls. He pulled-up his briches, headed to a nearby sign-making business, and had a large, neon-yellow decal put on the back window of the jeep that read *I Bought This Lemon At Bob Mcguire Chevrolet*.

It seems that the universe has a way of balancing itself out at times, and almost two years after the fact, I received a text from Danny. It was a picture of a newspaper article that read "Bob Macguire Chevrolet closes after thirty-six years." Now, I wasn't there in person to see Danny's initial reaction to the news, but I'm sure that there was a great big smile on his face as he likes to believe that he had something to do with their demise.

Danny's brilliance will be seen several times in the coming pages.

Greeny

Mike Green is another example of what makes the local watering hole is such a special place. Whether it was the constant threats to "take my butt," the time I caught him licking a magazine photo of Cristiano Ronaldo, or our disorienting night together dressed as drag queens in coconut bras and grass skirts, bartending with Mike was an absolute pleasure.

His story illustrates the close family ties that are often developed within the walls of the local drinking establishment. This die-hard Philadelphia Eagles and Manchester United supporter (and Ronaldo stalker) greets *every single guest* with an extended hand and an inviting hello.

He was not blessed with a closely-knit family. Instead, he's found tribal members at the watering hole—at lots of watering holes, in fact. When he walks into any one of his local spots, it takes him a while to get through all of the hugs and handshakes before he's able to take a sip of his drink.

Slinging drinks is a perfect gig for a social butterfly like Greeny. Within these confines, he has developed a diverse entourage of followers; from attractive, barely-legal girls to elderly chaps who still pride themselves on telling dick jokes. People love to be around him and he loves to be around people. He's a guy who gets it—the importance of genuine hospitality—plain and simple.

Art

Who doesn't adore a gigantic lumberjack with a love for beer and fast cars? I was lucky enough to bartend with such a creature a few years ago at the Irish pub. Despite many elbows to my jaw, rancid after-hours farts, crunched toes, and even a lacerated hand from the bottle of vodka he lobbed at me (which then shattered when it collided with the highball glasses I had cupped in my arms), he was a great guy to raise hell with.

Born and raised in Massachusetts, this avid Red Sox, Pats, and Bruins fan has bartended all over the country. And speaking of the Bruins, I'm sure he remembers quite well the night that he and I worked together when I single-handedly brought the Philadelphia Flyers back from a 3-0 deficit in game 7 of the playoffs in 2010 by summoning the awful powers of voodoo. That's right; I stuck 4 toothpicks into a leprechaun doll dressed as a Bruin's player. We won 4-3 to advance to the finals. Creepy, I know.

Art's humor, intelligence, and energy made him one of my favorite bartenders that I've ever had the pleasure of working with. I learned a lot from him—like how not to drag the garbage out at the end of the night. Tears streamed from our eyes and our abdominal muscles burned as we all crowded around a small computer screen to watch—over and over again—the surveillance video of the Paul Bunyan lookalike falling hard to kiss the ground.

One night, at the end of a shift, Art was dragging two garbage containers behind him, one in each hand, when his feet became entangled by a lingering plastic strap. Gravity took care of the rest. The tumble heard 'round the town ended with his head bouncing off of the concrete landing ramp outside of the back door. Thankfully, his beard cushioned the fall. He laid there for a moment—defeated—to figure shit out and to prepare himself for the imminent jokes that he knew were coming from us soon.

He was sought-out by the pub's ownership to "create an environment that he would like to spend time in recreationally." And so he did. The big guy was the mastermind behind what eventually turned into one of the most fun watering holes I've ever been to. Art ran trivia night, in which he was given a microphone and an complimentary bar tab. He made sure to get his fill as he belched out profanity, raunchy jokes, and burps over the sound system. His antics gained the loyalty of an entire room, which was completely packed every Wednesday night.

We dressed up in all sorts of costumes as Art hosted movie night, game night, and his specialty: blackout nights. Those tended to happen quite often whenever the big guy was slinging drinks.

But when you're about six-foot-six in height, someone is bound to want to take you down a peg or two. And so they did—incredibly unjustifiably—as the micro-managers who eventually drove the place into the rocks claimed another victim. He was exiled for turning the place into a playground —the exact thing he was hired to do in the first place. Once the Bostonian brute was gone, many battalions from his army of regulars never returned.

Cory

I remember the first time I met Cory. He was introduced to me by a manager as my trainee for the evening. He was to shadow me as I was to show him the ropes. It quickly seemed to me, however, that he had done this type of work once or twice before and didn't need much coaching.

We began bullshitting about work and play, and that's when I learned that, just like me, he's big into surfing. We exchanged pictures of us spending time with the same chick that we both happened to be in love with—Mother Ocean. His humility shined through initially, as he failed to inform me about his surf apparel company—*Jetty*—that he and some close friends owned and operated.

Corey is a great example of someone who sees more than just the social advantages of bartending, but also the entrepreneurial upside as well. As a drink slinger, you're able to pitch ideas to loads of enthused and seemingly interested guests. People tend to listen to the guy or gal pouring the drinks.

This young go-getter and former guest on ABC's *The Bachelorette* views his bartending shift as a way to market himself, as well as a way to enjoy himself. He'll pour some drinks for his guests and then give them a sticker or two— maybe even a shirt if they're lucky enough. This marketing tactic has worked well for his company as they are one of the larger surf apparel providers on the east coast with ambition to expand further to the west.

JettyLife.com. Go there. Buy clothes. Then get drunk and take them off.

Kat

Skill, compassion, wit, and grit—she's got it all.

Kathleen, like me, was a member of the original lineup at the Irish pub, not as a bartender, but as a hostess. It didn't really take long, however, for her to ascend the hierarchy of the watering hole and forge her identity as one of the best bartenders I've ever had the pleasure of working with.

A vagabond from a family of vagabonds, Kat spent most of her life on foreign soil—in particular, a patch in one of the most historically-preserved, tense, and dangerous areas in the world—the high-walled city of Jerusalem. Her father, chief journalist and correspondent at CBN news in Jerusalem and author of *Dateline Jerusalem*, moved the family to the Middle East for work when she was young. It quickly became her home.

A common tag-along on many of her father's trips to the front lines of Lebanon or the poverty-stricken slums of Mozambique, Kathleen was exposed the to complexities of the world at an extremely young age. Her short, black hair that falls to her shoulders, and her crystal-blue eyes qualify her as a *Coraline* lookalike—a label that suits her adventurous and curious spirit very well. She has a wider, more peripheral view of life than most bartenders (if not most people in general), and her passion to fight the good fight often shines through her work.

Her life's education, work, and aspirations are all centered around fixing the world. She believes that social work is her calling, and I can't help but agree given all of the strangers I've seen and heard spill their guts out to her. She often uses her platform as a bartender to listen to people's stories and then 'wow' them with her introspect and wisdom. I don't know how many times we had to shovel a guy or gal off of a bar stool at last call, the guest reluctant to end their therapy session after having such an emotional breakthrough.

Kat has the capability of impressing just about anyone with her intelligence and perspective, yet she knows how to throw down when need be. She can crank with the best of them, and is not unfamiliar with giving an unruly guest or two the ol' heave-ho. On one particularly testosterone-filled night while bartending at the Irish pub, a few drunk and obnoxious cops got all the shit-talk they could handle after they got mouthy with her once she flagged them. They left with their tails between their legs.

Joe

As a friend and business acquaintance to Cory, Joe is another example of someone who sees the marketing and networking opportunity that bartending can provide.

A surfer, philosophizer, dog-lover, and one of the most talented artists I've ever met, Mr. Hodnicki traveled the Caribbean after college using bartending and his art skills to pay for his adventures along the way. When he wasn't drawing or painting something badass, he could be found at the local watering hole pouring beers, serving up bar food, and cracking jokes with guests.

For fourteen years or so he worked as a barman, and during that time he made priceless connections that eventually landed him a large amount of the freelance art jobs that were available in town. If you're trying to market yourself in the creative world, every guest that sits down at your bar could be a potential partner or client. And he knew that well.

After impressing enough people with his work, he built a big enough following that would see him win the medal design contest for the 2012 Winter X-Games. That's right; go on Google and search "2012 Winter X-Games medal." There it is. Joe made that.

It was when he began to collaborate with me on this book—ideas and planned artwork—when apparel company Urban Outfitters scooped him up and made him a head designer. Since then, he's stepped away from the ranks of his fellow bartenders to allow him more time to work on his art.

Check out his website at sharingthestoke.com to see some rad paintings. Buy a few and then get drunk while looking at them on your wall.

Casey

It was always fun to watch Casey try to act tough and intimidate folks at the bar who maybe crossed the line with her. Most of the other drink slingers I've worked with had some bite to back up behind their bark. Casey, well, didn't necessarily have the sharpest teeth of my merry band of bartenders. And I mean that in the most complimentary way possible.

A history major with a love for good wine and dogs, she lacks a single mean bone in her body. I mean, there might be one or two of them floating around in there somewhere, but I have yet to encounter any. She was knighted into our Irish pub family the same way many others were—by drinking there first and getting to know everyone. Once we found out that she was interested in a hospitality gig, she was brought on board to sling drinks with the rest of us.

She took on the role of 'mom' for the most part, cleaning up after us when we'd lazily close the bar or scolding us for being inappropriate and "fresh." She did the same to all of the creepy old men who would surround her during her daytime shifts when they would solicit her to travel the world with them. I'd often work the dinner shift, and whenever I relieved her during happy hour, all of the old farts would immediately groan and complain. "Yeah, I know, I know," I would play along. "Casey's going home for the night. Fun's over. You poor saps are stuck with me now."

Laff

Working alongside this incredibly charismatic and intelligent barman they call "Laff" was a whirlwind of days and nights spent joking, complaining, and philosophizing. Being that he was a resident of the town in which I bartended, he'd often visit us at the Irish pub after a long bartending shift of his own at a place about twenty minutes away.

Tired and weary from a long day of double-majoring in school and pouring beers at night, he'd greet us at the bar with a friendly smile, take a sip of his beer, and then head outside for a smoke. By this time of the night, it was usually mellow enough for me to meander outside to join him.

Laff is a guy who really sees the beauty and novelty in slinging drinks. As a former corporate slave to the man, he was lucky and aware enough to be able to see where that path was leading him. He quickly escaped the corporate life and jumped behind the bar where he found his passion: people. Although, he'd argue that and probably say something snarky like "but, I fucking hate people—you know that," it's the truth.

We'd exchange stories about the characters we served that night and how our experiences tied into deeper psychological and sociological contexts. After a sip and a long drag from his cigarette, he'd exhale deeply, usually muttering a profound comment such as "I hate this job and love it just as much." It didn't take long before we really took a liking to him. As soon as we had an opening, we scooped him up, strapped a kilt on him, and made him one of us.

An old soul with great adoration for classic literature and film, Ryan is the kind of person that *makes* a pub. He's the guy who epitomizes a neighborhood bartender. He laughs the loudest and is the most unforgiving of his mistakes and shortcomings. His sharp wit and seemingly endless energy supply kept the room going until there were no more. And once there literally were no more and the bar was closed down for the night, he'd head on home to finish grading papers for the class he was training to be a teacher in. He had a work ethic that few people could match, and could sing better Johnny Cash than Johnny Cash's Johnny Cash.

Teen

Known for her sarcasm as much as her porn-caliber orgasm scream she'd immediately blast over the microphone once the bar had been closed for the night, Teenie was a true gem to work with. And for.

It's not often that a friend becomes a boss and it works so well. We'd start our shift with a friendly hello and a story or two about the night prior, and a few hours later, I'd find myself getting chewed-out for allowing an army of maggots to fester in the salt rimmer because I had neglected to clean it out. I'd apologize to her by rolling the blunt or pouring the beers at Danny's place after work that night. Her skill, knowledge, and influence was not to be underestimated, and I understood that.

A party-starter by trade, she knew how to instigate a good time. On any given weeknight at the pub, Teenie was known to disappear for an hour, and then return with bags upon bags of party favors from the local costume shop. We'd all dress-up in the most ridiculous outfits we could create, don our glowsticks, turn down the lights, crank-up the techno music, and throw ourselves (and those who weren't scared away already) an all-out rave. She'd often bring the coffee, candy, water guns, and always—the good time.

Teenie was the parental figure of the pub—a friend to all of us—yet our boss and our disciplinarian. She was much respected at the pub and throughout the community, yet that proved to be not enough for the powers that (used to) be. She, just like Art and many other pub all-stars after her, were exiled without much reason. We never recovered from her absence.

Noteworthy and Mentionable

And then, there were the rest. Some, I worked with and can barely remember their names. Others left a bigger footprint on my memory via the beers we drank, money we gambled, engaging talks we had, passion-filled rants about some asshole we served that night, unruly guests we 86'd, bongs we ripped, or saliva we swapped together.

There was **Brandon**, the 6'4" gangster black guy who is gay as the night is long but you would never know it at first. Anytime I bent over to get beer out of the cooler behind the bar, he would stand behind me, grunt, and say something like "Damn, Jay...I'd break you in half, son." Plead with him I would: "Please don't. I have my rape whistle and am not afraid to use it."

There was **Gerard**, a former Marine grunt who stood beside me as some clown—dressed in his working Air Force uniform—berated us on how we apparently "take advantage of service members." Even after telling the dude that we were both prior military, he continued his drunken slur as he staggered out the front exit, Gerry and I both giggling and also feeling a little confused.

Pete, who at the time was acting GM, hired me at the Italian joint. We'd sit there after hours until the sun came up drinking Grand Marnier neat and talking shit about the crazy owner of the place and how likely it was that the Feds would come kicking the door down any minute in search of the cracked-out wannabe mob boss.

Robbie, who was just recently named one of Miami's most influential bartenders, showed me how to pour a Long Island by putting four bottles in one hand. Still to this day I can't properly do it (probably due to the many fingers and knuckles I've broken in sports).

The PG-rated version of **Swallace** once called his ex-boss' house at 4am, and when his wife picked up, he shouted "Hey! Is this -----'s house? Well tell him that I said that he's a huge *CUNT!*" Working with Swallace was always hilarious. The hardest thing about slinging drinks with this guy was not laughing in the middle of a guest's drink or food order with all of the *extremely* grotesque and inappropriate things being whispered in my direction. These "things" often were in relation to some form of sodomy or defecation.

Dennis is an old-school, quick-witted, no-time-for-nonsense bartending grandmaster who has seen it all a few times over. In his upper-50s, he has the comedic response time of a young stand-up, my favorite line of his coming on the day of the Kentucky Derby when he took a request from a customer: "Can you make me a Mint Julep?" "No—we have a lot of great bourbon; I don't want to ruin it with mint."

There was **a guy** (can't remember his name) who used to pop a shit-ton of pills before a shift and yap his face off to one or two guests and pretty much ignore the rest of the guests at the watering hole. Now, this would be acceptable if he was hustling them and it resulted in a gigantic tip that we would split. But no, usually he would just creep them out with his constant grinding of his teeth and profuse sweating.

Loretta did the same amount of talking to guests as the prior guy, but the difference was that she made huuuuge contributions to our tip bucket. Her good looks and quick, witty personality made it so that I was always able to pay my bills on time.

Ian, who holds multiple college degrees, is highly-intelligent craft beer and cocktail connoisseur who, after dealing with a difficult guest, could often be heard muttering "I'm going to make him/her cry tonight."

Kyle is a Chicago Blackhawks fan, and therefore, he's a huge asshole.

Alexa, whom I only worked with several times before I was shit-canned from the Irish pub, is a tall, athletic, pretty blonde with loads of sarcasm and wit. You may have seen her work on *The Angry Bartender's* Facebook page, in fact, as she ever-so-gently portrayed some generic asshats and douchebags that bartenders are likely to encounter over a lengthy tenure of slinging drinks. The video is up on Youtube, titled "The Bartender's Perception." Check it out.

Bobby's claim to fame is his poetic execution of the tidal wave shot. It's his specialty, and for good reason. He doesn't give a shit if your smartphone is on the bar or if you spent twenty minutes greasing up your fohawk—if you ask him to make you something special, he will certainly deliver, sometimes in the form of a small shot glass of warm, house vodka on the bar...and then a wave of water to the face. That's right—whoever got mouthy that night or was sold out by their friends on a birthday was drenched—Shamu-style—by Bobby and his bucket o' water.

Mary's intelligence, blue eyes, sass, and obsession over Maynard James Keenan of *Tool* made it impossible to have a boring shift with her. She's a character that seems to fall into many categories, and yet, none at all. She's one of the most unique people I've ever had the pleasure of serving, working with, and having drunken adventures with—like the night we got wasted in Philadephia and drew over one-hundred cartoons of penises to be hidden in her roommates' apartment.

Erin is as gritty as they come. Most of her bartending experience consisted of serving em' up at the Jersey shore during the summer on Long Beach Island. The 'joisey shoah' can be a challenging place to work for even the most patient of drink slingers, but in Erin's case, she realized it was a waste of time to have patience. She threw people out for being too wasted, not tipping enough, or just because she didn't like their face. Her rough around the edges style and ruthless, Jersey Shore-like aggressiveness proved to be a little too much at our Irish pub, and she eventually got her pink slip. Whatever, she belongs in stand-up comedy anyway.

7

Happy Hour

In the later afternoon hours, the watering hole quickly became crowded with frequenters. I sensed a collective rambunctiousness throughout the room as the herd grew larger by the minute. And then the feeding frenzy began. Everyone looked like they had arrived directly from their jobs, and appeared to be extremely thirsty and malnourished. They grabbed at baskets full of french fries, fought for plates covered in chicken wings, and desperately washed it all down with glasses full of alcohol. The scene was intense. It must have been a long day at the office.

***

Today was a hard day. Your boss is having problems at home so he takes it out on you with more criticism than usual. As you turn out of the workplace, you hear strange noises coming from the engine of your car accompanied by an awful burning odor that sifts through the vents. And, to top it all off, you are reminded by your lovely wife that you said you would clean the gutters tonight. Well, guess what—your boss is out of your life until tomorrow morning, your car made it to the tavern just fine, and there's no rain in the forecast for the next four days—the gutters can wait. You've arrived at the watering hole. Take a load off. You've earned it.

The band Loverboy at least got *one* lyric right during their music career: "Everybody's workin' for the weekend." That sweet smell of freedom snakes out of the local watering hole and into the noses of stressed and overworked employees across the land. It calls to them like mythological sirens and fills their spirits with relief and hope before inevitably guiding them to instant bliss in a glass.

It's happy hour, people! The time has come to loosen up those ties, gripe about your boss' incessant micromanaging, and take advantage of those cheap drink and food specials before having to pick the kids up from soccer practice. While bar guests are munching on half-priced apps, guzzling down domestic drafts, and singing along to the hymns of Neil Diamond or Journey, the evening bartending shift is just beginning.

Happy hour usually includes an eclectic collection of characters, all of whom arrived for the same reason—to get a buzz. It's likely to be the only time of the day—and only place for that matter—where a carpenter will be seated next to an accountant, who is seated next to an army captain, fully dressed in work clothes, buzzed and singing aloud to *'Don't Stop Believin'.* Add in a Native American chief with a headdress and you have the perfect lineup for a Village People cover band.

I think it's safe to assume that many or even most of those who work for a living seriously dislike their jobs. And when they walk into the doors of their local Chili's, go-go joint, or Irish pub, the troubles and anxieties they carried with them throughout the day are left at the door. These worker ants are on vacation at this moment in time, away from their respective colonies of monotonous nail hammering and paper stacking. They're ready to toast to each other—to another day on the grind—and to getting a buzz on. It's a very happy time indeed!

The hour of happiness usually begins around 3 or 4pm, but sometimes seems to extend itself until closing time—15 beers, multiple shots, and several dignity-lowering incidents later. There is something about that initial buzz that gets you. It really sucks you in and can defeat the willpower and productivity of even the most self-disciplined go-getter. After a hard-fought day spent slaving away to the man, that bubbly, euphoric feeling that follows a few beers can tickle the soul and leave you wanting more.

Happy hour can be ultra-seductive. If you don't watch yourself, you won't be on time to pick up the kids or meet your wife at couple's therapy. Instead, you'll find yourself being poked by the bartender's broomstick in an attempt to stop you from drowning in your own drool as your head lays passed out on the bar at last call.

The only thing better than happy hour, of course, is happy hour on a Friday. At the Irish pub, we used to gave away a $200 gift card every Friday at the end of happy hour. With each plate of food, whether an appetizer or entrée, came a raffle ticket. Once 7pm rolled around, we picked a ticket and announced the lucky winner. It was a great way to rile up the natives as well as draw the interest of first-time visitors.

Most people who came in for the happy hour drawing ended up leaving shortly after the winning ticket was revealed.

Usually, the winner paid their tab and left, saving the gift card for a few dinners and drinks out in the future. However, there were always those who stayed. They now had $200.00 in bar currency to spend on themselves and fellow working class heroes trying to extend recess just a little while longer.

Fuckin' Happy Hour

Two police officers sat down at my bar one afternoon at around 5:30-6pm on a Friday evening. After I served them their first round of drinks, which ended up as a Miller lite and a Smithwicks, I asked them if they would like to start a tab—normal procedure. The answer was a definitive, simultaneous, and seemingly choreographed *NO*, but they requested a menu so they could order an appetizer to split. One and done was the plan.

When their order came through, I placed their raffle ticket in front of them and explained how the giveaway worked. They seemed uninterested but held onto the ticket anyway. I was pretty busy at the bar—not in the weeds—but busy enough to overlook their order and not realize that after twenty minutes, it still wasn't in front of them. I apologized to them both and bought their next round.

As soon as I placed the shot glasses in front of them— placeholders which signified that they had two drinks coming to them—their food appeared over their shoulder delivered by the food runner. They practically inhaled their grub, and because I was now offering to fill up their glasses once more at no charge, they decided they'd stay just a little while longer.

It was now time to bump someone up into the next tax bracket by making them $200 richer in bar currency. Some people make a point to buy five or six items to increase their chances of winning, as others just nibble on one plate of chicken wings and pray that their one ticket does the job. On this day, it was the lone plate that won out.

I notified the two officers, both in their mid-30s, that they had just won the $200 gift card. They looked at me confusedly and asked me to repeat myself.

"214, right? (I'm totally making those numbers up. My memory isn't *that* good) You guys won! Congrats!"

I don't think they had payed much attention to me when I explained why I was giving them the ticket in the first place, so it appeared that they were still unclear as to what was going on.

"You guys just won the drawing!"

Once I handed them the gift card they finally began to react.

"Hah, I guess we're staying then," said the one guy reluctantly, but with a bit of excitement.

"Fuck yeah we are!" howled the other.

They stayed, ate, drank, and met a sarcastic, witty, and extremely sassy group of women—all teachers at a local high school who had just finished another stressful week full of bratty, snotty kids. The now loaded chivalrous men ended up buying drinks for them all night. By 9pm, they had moved closer to each other, playing musical chairs in an attempt to sniff each other out. By 10 pm, they were doing body shots off of each other. By 11pm the kings of the raffle were pressuring me to do body shots off of their new and busty friends. With a raised eyebrow, I sighed "eh, duty calls." I dove right in.

At 12am, their tab was over $300.00. They had turned the bar into a real banger of a party, buying drinks for total strangers while I sat back and enjoyed *their* show. They were all drunken messes, yapping away about God knows what. Apart from a few other stragglers, it was only them left in the bar as last call began to creep up on us.

At 1am, the alpha had made his intentions known. He was now face-to-face with his targeted piece of ass for the evening, whispering onion ring and Guinness-flavored sweet nothings into her ear. The beta was now passed out on the bar, sitting up straight, arms and hands hanging in mid-air with his forehead resting on the bar top. As I covered him in a blanket of linens and placed a squishy, stuffed basketball under his head as a pillow, we all sang "rockabye baby" to him and took pictures that would surely be used as ball-busting material at the station.

While this was taking place, the alpha wouldn't wait any longer to have his prey. He said something to his busty babe that made her sass back "Oh yeah? Will you wrestle me down and frisk me?"

Her friends were too busy trying to look up my kilt that I occasionally wore to work to notice that the alpha was taking their friend away like a leopard dragging an antelope up into its tree to eat. I have *zero* doubt that they went and fucked in the bathroom. I thought *Eh, whatever—Let em' hump.* I blasted a little Marvin Gaye over the speakers to help set the mood.

They both made it back a few minutes later, completely disheveled with smirks on their faces. While the woman tried to deny the drunken accusations of her heckling friends, the alpha looked at me—wobbling and cross-eyed with a great big smile—her lip gloss smeared all over his face and neck. Ah, the evidence trail of glitter makeup products—it will nail you every time.

As he woke his sleeping partner up, I handed them their tab. I'll never forget his grumpy response as he was awakened from his slumber. "Mmmmfuckin' happy hour."

It seemed like this had happened before in their prior watering hole adventures. "Fuckin' happy hour," I replied. I thanked them for making my night a memorable one and watched them climb into a passenger van that one of them had called for pick-up duty. *Fuckin happy hour*, I mumbled to myself once more with a smile as I started cleaning up.

8

Last Call

By this point in the evening, only a few stranglers remained. It was late, and many of the natives had already completed their replenishment for the night and vacated the premises to mate and/or hibernate.

The carnage that sprawled from wall to wall was a testimonial to the wild frenzy that took place throughout the day. Broken glass, peanut shells, crumbled paper, shredded coasters, bits of food, spilled drinks, vomit, and even lost articles of clothing littered the grounds once last call was announced by the bartenders.

I documented some amazing and disturbing things once the herd of natives was being forced out of the area, such as a fist fight between two gigantic men, and a strip tease amongst two older women—a plethora of bare skin that was more alarming than the blood spilled during the fisticuffs. It appeared to me that last call was the dinner bell that sounded to the primal being that lay dormant in the DNA code of the 9-5, working human being. Last call was the frequenters' last opportunity to get their fix, and they certainly did with a heavy dose of urgency.

***

Finally! Thank the gods! It's that magical hour of the evening (or morning) that bartenders across the world yearn to be greeted by. It's last call—the final opportunity for the natives of the watering hole to fill their glasses once more with their preferred booze. It also means that, in mere minutes, the bar staff will be able to toast to the night and enjoy the sweet taste of the drink that they have been pouring for their patrons all night long.

Last call is a call to action for both sides of the bar, both guests and bartenders. My side is concerned with getting paid and kicking everyone out before the whole show turns into a pumpkin. The other side is usually hell-bent on getting one more drink, finding a piece of ass for the night, and more importantly, figuring out, in quite a drunken state, how to click the pen they were given by the bartender and legibly sign their credit card slips.

OK, the time is upon us, but how do you inform the masses that it's last call? You can just yell *last call*, right? Of course. That usually works fine. But if you want everyone out in a hurry, there are more effective and creative approaches that bartenders like to deploy.

Beer goggles, which is a term that represents the dangerous and rapid decline of standard in relation to sexual attraction, are worn by the majority of the scavengers who remain at the watering hole at last call. An advanced pair of beer goggles can make you want to hump a fire hydrant, or even take *Deloris* home despite her drunken incoherence, red wine stains on her teeth, and the smell of vomit on her breath.

To combat the resilience of beer goggle wearers, we find that the most useful (and abrupt) way of ending the night at the drinking hole is to shock the crowd with our timeless friend—bright, artificial light. That's right; 20,000 volts of obnoxious fluorescent shine will scare anyone out of the bar who is even slightly self-conscious of their appearance or their chance to score that night. We refer to these blinding beams as the *ugly lights.*

The ugly lights do what the name implies—they make you appear ugly. Every blemish, pimple, and herpes outbreak will be highlighted and easily visible by the person or people you're trying to mate with that night. Cruel, I know.

But we're not *that* cruel. We usually announce to everyone that the few minutes that remain before we deploy the ugly lights will be the last chance for those who consider themselves even remotely ugly to escape through the exits unnoticed. Once the lights are illuminated, most of those brave enough to stick around end up scattering like raccoons that were digging through garbage cans and spooked by motion-detecting spotlights.

When blinding light doesn't work, we resort to disturbing noises, insults, or both. We blast Red Peters' *The Closing Song* and sing along to his lyrics "Get the fuck out of here, finish up that beer," all while reminding those who remain to pay their tabs, because if not, we'll be inclined to use their credit cards to buy some type of kinky, online Asian porn.

If they still don't get the hint and stubbornly remain semi-conscious on their barstool, clinging on the to the few drops of booze that swish around in their glass, I personally like to use *The Most Annoying Sound in the World* YouTube clip from the movie *Dumb and Dumber* on repeat, at the highest volume that the bar speakers can handle. That's ten minutes of continuous, deafening screeching. It's always comical when a drunken native or two come staggering over and try yelling at the top of their lungs for me to turn it off. I facetiously yell back "Turn it up? I can't! It's already as loud as it goes!" The scavengers pleading and feigning for that last shot or beer usually get the hint by that point. It's time to go, people. All things—good and bad—must come to an end.

The Primordial Hour

Last call often proves to be the hour of the untamed. Words never intended on being shared with the world have a tendency of escaping through loose lips. At this time of the night, many frequenters' subconscious selves are at maximum strength. Some are exuberant and celebratory, others are reckless and confrontational. Often times, however, they're sad and heartbroken.

As bartenders, we look forward to closing time in the same way teachers look forward to the school bell sounding sweet freedom from their energy-sucking students. Yet, once in a while, even teachers see a bittersweet aspect to the immediate evaporation of pubescent monsters—especially if they know that they face problems at home.

Bartenders often play the role of rodeo clowns trying to corral those who are bucking out of control, and at the end of a long and rambunctious night, we just want everyone to go the fuck home. The arguments, drunken spills, loud music, fights, complaints, bad tippers, and relentless barrage of bad cliches and jokes have a way of pushing us to the brink. *Drink em' up! Get the fuck out!*

There arise certain occasions, however, when as a drink slinger, you find yourself feeling deflated and empathetic as you watch a guest leave. It's so easy to get caught up in the wild rumpus of the night out at the watering hole and sometimes forget that the majority of guests—the good ones—are sitting on your barstools to get away from it all and to metaphorically exhale after a long day or week.

They come to see *you*—a bartender, of all people, and desire a beer and to rid themselves of the anxiety that's been plaguing them. They're trying to climb out of the swirling toilet bowl of despair that they've slowly been drowning in. They crave human interaction. They need some type of release or to make a connection with another creature that has no relation or direct connotation to what it is that's bothering them. A lot of bartenders tend to forget or mindfully ignore that. I know I do.

A Scotsman Walks Into A Bar

I once was greeted by a guest at the Irish pub who appeared to be in a depressed state from the get-go. It was a fairly slow, yet strange night—a Tuesday or Wednesday perhaps, and there were guests scattered throughout the bar. He claimed a seat a few spots down from where I was bullshitting with another guest or two. I watched him laboriously remove his overcoat, hat, scarf, and gloves. I thought nothing of his painful wincing given that it was the middle of winter in New Jersey.

Once I greeted him, it took him quite a while to shake off his thousand-yard stare and acknowledge me, his hands folded in a chapel shape in front of his face covering his nose and mouth.

"How you doin', sir? What can I do for ya?"

"Can I have a Guinness, please," he requested in a thick Scottish brogue.

"Absolutely. Menu?"

"No. A Whiskey, though. I'd like one of those too."

"Well, we have a lot of that...anything in particular?"

"I trust you."

I began pouring his beer, and as I let it settle for a minute as per Guinness law, I began to analyze him. I watched him as his hands—still folded—slid down his face, squished his nose, and eventually dragged over his lips. As I finished his beer and placed it in front of him alongside his shot of Powers, I saw two half-dried streaks of water on his face, partially wiped and evaporated. He had been crying. *What the fuck*, I thought as I turned around to start him a tab. *More drama. Great.*

The night had already proven to be mentally exhausting. Between the difficult women I had during happy hour who sent back three out of four drinks, to the five-percent tip I got on a $200 tab after buying them a round and performing a solo rendition of 'happy birthday' for one of them, to crushing my finger between kegs while switching out taps earlier in the evening, I wasn't in the mood to go above-and-beyond anymore. I wanted last call to rear its hiding head. I wanted to go home.

At about thirty minutes before 1am, the crowd of natives began to retire for the evening. As they closed their tabs one by one, the Scottish fellow's glass became empty. I was hoping that he'd be done for the night as well.

"How you holding up? Would you like another?"

"Yes please—one more of each. Please."

It was in that response that I detected a real problem. This guy wasn't upset because his favorite team lost, nor was he tearing-up from the aroma of red onion leftover on an adjacent plate that I was about to bus. After I poured him his next round and placed the drinks in front of him, I thought I'd see what was up. At this point, last call was about twenty minutes away.

"So I'm not going to ask you how your day has been...it's pretty obvious that you're having a shitty one..."

"Heh," he exhaled strongly as he shook his head and cricked his neck. "What lead you on?" A lone drop of water began to slide down his cheek.

"Yeah, it's just that it's a Tuesday...and it's almost last call... and you're alone...and you've been crying...and I haven't seen you in here before...and I work here...a lot."

"I came here to kill my mother."

Um, what?

My eyes got wide and I took a step back as I thought I had just gotten a murderer to open up to me. It's not every day someone confesses to you that they just killed someone.

"Easy, lad. It's not like that. I came here from Scotland to take my mother off of life support."

Whew! At least this guy wasn't here to end a killing spree by slaughtering the bartender at last call 'No Country for Old Men' style.

"Sorry to hear that," I said softly as I nervously and anxiously wiped the bar surface around him. That's what bartenders do when we're anxious or uncomfortable—we clean stuff. It's often a defense mechanism. So if you ever find yourself spilling your guts out to your drink slinger and it seems odd that he's cleaning everything three times over as you talk, you might want to activate your filter.

A tiny seedling of a soft spot began to grow inside of my heart which had been frozen that night from all of the assholes I had encountered. His thick Scottish accent—an accent that much of my family still speaks with—reminded me of them. I could tell that he wanted to talk about it but had the social competency to restrain himself from being "that guy." I don't think he wanted to be the one poor sap sitting on a barstool alone at last call, telling the bartender all of his problems.

I encouraged him by asking vague questions like "How long are you here for," and "What part of Scotland are you from?" Soon, the floodgates were open.

"I bury her in two days' time," he told me as he brought his shot glass to his mouth and swigged the rest of his whiskey. "Then I go back home. I've got a lot of shit I need to figure out."

"I noticed that you said *I* bury her...is it just you?"

"Aye. Aye it is. I'm an only child. My father died years and years ago. Since then...just my mother and I."

"Do you have any cousins or anything?"

"I did. Two of them. Small family. One of them lives in Australia, but I lost touch with her years ago. The other passed away as well." He looked down, and then looked at me—his eyes resembling buckets of water being filled to the brim and about to spill over. I can still remember that moment like it was this morning.

I saw that he was becoming overwhelmed with emotion, so I decided to ask him more questions about Scotland. We made small-talk about what he did for a living as well as sports and movies. It turned out that he was a big Glasgow Rangers fan—a team and fan base traditionally backed by the Protestant population of Scotland and beyond. The *Huns* were and still are hated by their neighbors by a few kilometers, Glasgow Celtic. Celtic is the Catholic side of the coin—one backed by most of my family. I busted his balls a bit and told him that I was at the very last game they played each other in April of 2012. Celtic won 3-0, and Rangers was soon banished to relegation after going bankrupt.

After a brief period of friendly bantering, he told me that his parents moved to the states when he was 19, leaving him behind in Scotland. It instilled in him a feeling of abandonment that most children wrestle with when their parents immigrate to new lands to find work without them.

"Why did they leave Scotland?"

"They wanted to get in on the real estate boom happening at the time. They sold their business in Scotland and bought one over here. Then they started buying houses and properties."

"Well, if you don't mind me asking, why didn't *you* come here too?"

"I'll answer that question if I could have one last drink."

His eyes were now a bit drier but his cheeks were puffed-out like the egg on Hasim Rahman's forehead after he fought Evander Holyfield. As I poured his Guinness, he climbed off of his stool and headed towards the restroom to take a leak. As I closed-out the check of the last remaining couple at the bar and wished them a good night, I realized that it was 1:35am—five minutes past last call.

"I got caught up in your story and didn't realize that last call was five minutes ago. Can I get you anything else before I close your tab?"

"I'd like to buy *you* a drink if I could."

Like stated in other parts of this book, we're not really supposed to drink behind the bar—at least in most establishments. *Fuck it*, I thought. I couldn't leave him hanging out to dry. I took him up on his offer but didn't add it to his check. I poured shots for both of us while urging him to continue his story.

"I was angry at them for wanting to leave home and I fought them on it. But their mind was set. They obviously wanted to bring me, but I had a wee bird (girlfriend) at the time, and I really wanted to show them that I didn't need them, and that I could be just as successful as them—without their help. It was the rock n' roll, rebellious side of me."

"To rising up," I joked as I clinked my glass to his. Of course, it would just so happen that it went down the wrong pipe and I started coughing up a lung.

133

"Christ...you Americans..."

"It went down...*cough*...the wrong...*cough*...pipe...*cough*...I swear."

He began to chuckle as he watched me gasping for air. I laughed too. Then I noticed that he didn't even look at his check when I presented it to him. He simply slid cash in between the padded covers of the black check presenter and pushed it back towards me. "Just keep whatever's left."

"Thanks. So, you think you'll be OK?"

"Ahh, I know I'll be OK. But there's something I want to say to you before I leave you be for the night. You have a soap box handy?"

"Haha. Here we go. Lemme guess—go Rangers?"

"No. Well, yes. But seriously...tell your parents...your family...your friends...even complete strangers...tell them that you love them. The last time I talked to my fiancé was right before she was killed in a car wreck years ago. We were arguing—well, *I* was arguing about how I didn't like how she had to travel so much for work. The last time I talked to her, I told her that I was thinking about calling the whole thing off, even though it was my own selfish way of trying to get her attention. She probably took her last breath thinking that I didn't love her anymore."

I stood there in complete silence. Bartenders have always been known to be good pillows to cry on or unlicensed shrinks to debate your life's dilemmas with before you march home and drunkenly confront them. Sometimes I surprise myself with whatever borrowed philosophical advice that comes flowing out of my mouth and into the receptive mind of a guest. Other times, however, I freeze. I don't have anything of value to say, no advice to give. I feel like a hack. It was such on this night. I had absolutely nothing to say to him.

As I looked up at the clock—both to see the time and to subtly make him aware that he needed to leave—he continued. Five minutes until 2am.

"I know I have to leave, and I'm sorry to have kept you so long, but let me finish. Before my parents left, I told my father that I hated him. We had an argument about something so stupid that I can't even remember what it was, but all of the anger I had inside of me for them moving to the states came out. I never spoke to him again. He died from a heart attack a year after arriving here."

He put his coat, scarf, hat, and gloves back on, looked up at the clock, and continued. 1:58am.

"And my mother...she was trying to get me to move here to the states to take over her real estate businesses, but after all these years of trying to prove myself and my independence, I've distanced myself. I said no and sort of insinuated that it was her fault that my father passed. I told her that if they just stayed put in Scotland and worked at their own, small shop, Dad wouldn't have been so stressed. He wouldn't have had a heart attack."

He finished the last few drops of his beer as more water began to swell in his eyes. "My mother and I had that argument two weeks ago. She had a stroke later that night and was immediately brain dead. I got the call as her only remaining kin, and arrived a few days ago. I said my goodbyes, and signed off on removing her from life support. I killed her earlier today."

I stood there speechless still. I had nothing to say. What could I have said? *Man, that sucks?* I had nothing. I was shell-shocked. 1:59am.

"I'll walk you out," I said somberly.

As we arduously made our way towards the front exit, I tried to conjure something—*anything* worth saying to this guy before he took off. And yet, I remained speechless.

He shook my hand and pleaded me to remember what he said. I smiled graciously (at least that's what I think—it probably looked like I had gas), and thanked him for his visit. I asked him if he needed a taxi, to which he denied and told me that he was staying at the hotel up the street.

"No. Thank *you*. You made me laugh. I can't thank you enough for that," he said as he firmly shook my hand. "C'mon the Rangers."

"C'mon the hoops," I rebounded quickly. "Take care of yourself."

I locked the doors and then watched him walk across the parking lot until his figure was lost in the darkness and fog of the early morning.

It took me a lot longer to clean up and close that night, as I was mentally clouded and drained. I normally listen to reggae, jazz, or something relaxing after such a long and taxing night, but I performed my duties in silence. Just before sitting down and running the numbers for the evening, I suddenly realized that I still hadn't closed the Scotsman's check. I walked over to the bar to collect the booklet with his tab in it, and was aghast when I opened it and found a one hundred-dollar bill. His tab was a little over $30.

I was extra critical of myself as I got into my car and started the drive home that night. I'd say that I'm normally quite witty—even long-winded at times, yet I could barely get a word out to this guy. I must have sounded like someone being talked to who was in the middle of a heated game of *Call of Duty: Uh, huh. Yeah. Right. Yep. Oh, wow.*

Bartending is a timeless role, one that fits into many categories and none at all. Sure, at times we perform duties that a monkey could execute: pour beers, shake martinis, and help folks decide on a burger or a steak. Many bartenders are underachievers, compulsive gamblers, sex addicts, and alcoholics who will creatively ponder—for hours —different ways to dispose of the dead body of a guest who didn't tip. We often have ugly tattoos, small checking accounts, and a boatload of debt. Many of us are fuck-ups, plain and simple.

But we give great high-fives, hugs, and kisses, too. We listen, laugh—with you and at you—and can talk shit until the surface temperature of our opponent's skin heats up from all of the burns. The crooked paths we've taken and our deranged life choices have delivered us to the obscure, strange outskirts of the world and back again, full of drunken stories and unforgettable experiences shared with fellow humans. It's the kind of role that many responsibility-challenged misfits flock to.

It could be said that bartenders are addicts of the moment— the now; the time spent in the present connecting with good people while drinking good beer. For many of us, our impulsive nature has us clinging onto those moments of exhilaration, fighting tooth and nail to avoid letting them slip into memory. Singular and unique moments of euphoria and beauty and electrified human connection have us forgetting about the future quite often, for those things matter not when you're in the company of good people. And when we're at work behind the stick, we're often surrounded by good people. This is why some folks say that they'll stop bartending after college, but remain in the biz into their 40s, 50s, and beyond.

My encounter with this spiritually-bruised Scotsman is an example of such an electrified moment. When I yell *last call*, it's usually with a type of long-awaited sigh of relief—like letting an underpants-splitting fart *rip* after saying goodnight to a new boyfriend or girlfriend when you drop them off from the movies that evening. But on this particular night at the watering hole, I wanted the moment to extend. I wished it could have lasted a bit longer so that I could have maybe said something of importance—so that I could have been the witty bartender with Jeti-Gandalf wisdom. But it didn't. It ended just like any other sixty-second span of time. It ended with me softly urging the guy out the door. I wished there was something more I could do.

One Final Thought: Last Call

If it's drama that you seek, you'll likely find a decent amount —and then some—during the primordial hour at the local watering hole: last call. It's a small window of time that can encompass a wide range of strange behavior: unruly, hilarious, and sad. Last call is a spectacle of the human psyche and it's interactive traits. But no matter how much you want to stay, or how much *we* want *you* to stay, ya gotta go the fuck home.

9

Conflict

Ding…Ding…Ding! It's fight time! Alphas and betas alike clash as the rest of the bar frequenters look on anxiously. Verbal warnings are given, refreshments are thrown, clothing is torn, fists fly, and blood is spilled quite often at local drinking establishments during a bustling night out.

Throughout my time studying the wild, I've noticed that nature's watering holes often play host to some of the most shocking conflicts between rival creatures. It's the ecosystem that exhibits the most unpredictable behavior from such a diverse collection of guests. It makes for great entertainment.

Since beginning this study, I've noticed that there are lots of similarities between conflict in the wild and conflict at the bipedal drinking establishment. From what I've seen thus far, most of it has to do with mating rituals. That's right, men want a hole to stick it in and women want to breed young.

Admittedly, the interaction between male and female, male and male, female and female, transgendered and transgendered, etc., is wrapped-up in lots of different layers of social norms. Humans are generally polite to each other because it's socially encouraged. But make no mistake—our bodily instincts all trying to procreate whether we consciously want to or not. Sometimes, that desire breeds competition. Competition paired with alcohol breeds conflict. And here at the watering hole, there's plenty of both.

* * *

Willy makes the point that booze tends to be found at the scene of many fights—in and out of the barroom. More often than not, when police officers respond to a domestic disturbance at a trailer park somewhere in Oaklahoma, they have to step over piles of crushed Budweiser cans before they question anyone about who started what.

At the bar, booze has a way of turning people mad. Whether it's an argument amongst opposing fans about the call at home plate, a shoving match between two women who had the same choice in sundresses that night, or an all-out rock em' sock em' bar fight; when you cram drunken adults into a room together, fightin' words, dirty looks, and right hooks will eventually be exchanged.

Ringside Seats

As a bartender, our working environment provides us with ringside seats to some of the most awkward and vicious conflicts that occur between friends, family, and complete strangers alike. Eavesdropping is part of the job description. We're always on high alert for subtle clues as to how the pork chop came out of the kitchen or if the fries are too cold. If a guest's glass is about one-third of the way full, should you push another drink on them? Is this a heated conversation about religion or politics that could turn ugly?

141

Listening in and spying on guests is the best way to provide optimal service and to prevent anything bad from happening.

Bartenders are nosy and it's our duty to be that way. For matters of safety and guest satisfaction, we have to be vigilant and pay very close attention to detail. Some folks transform into Jeffery Dahmer after a few whiskeys, so it's important to identify potential threats that lay dormant on the premises. It's when we're on high alert that it's common to overhear embarrassing and gross conversations about yeast infections or instances of erectile dysfunction.

But it sucks when our job morphs into that of a boxing referee or wildlife control. We're there to make money doing something that we enjoy, but if we don't implement a certain level of control in the room, we'll find ourselves jumping over the bar to break up a brawl.

People fight at bars. We know this. But why are they more prone to do it at the watering hole than at the mall or movie theater?

Hollywood

Bar fights are highly entertaining in the movies. You know how they go: one guy says something raunchy to another guy's gal and before you know it, they're exchanging punches like Adam Sandler and Bob Barker in *Happy Gilmore*. Hollywood shows us some dude lunging at his dance partner with a broken bottle or someone being drug across the bar-top by a grizzly guy sporting a mullet—against his will he is escorted on his belly down the full length of the bar hitting every beer mug and bowl of peanuts that rests in his way.

The karate movie *Best of the Best* had a good bar fight scene. So did *Knockaround Guys, The Replacements, Roadhouse, Desperado,* and my personal favorite, Steven Segal's dance with all of Richie's boys in *Out for Justice.* This bloody barroom brawl blossoms into a beautiful ballet of broken bones, smashed furniture, insults, and missing teeth compliments of *Gino* as he searches for a wanted drug kingpin. "Anybody seen Richieeee?!" *Wham!*

In real life, though, bar fights are dangerous, costly, and typically avoidable. They usually occur as a result of a miniscule misunderstanding. After a few drinks, you catch someone eyeing you up—at least, you *think* they're eyeing you up. Realistically, they're looking past your thick head at the basketball game that's being televised on the screen behind you. As you both simultaneously make your way to the patio of the bar to have a smoke, you say something along the lines of "Yo...there a reason why you were lookin' at me all hard in there?" He responds sarcastically and confesses that he has no idea what you're talking about. You accuse him again. He gets defensive and raises his voice. Sure enough, tensions escalate, and before you know it, you're bouncing your knuckles off of each other's skulls. This happens a lot.

What you don't see on TV, however, is the guy who's trying to break-up the fight getting tagged in the midst of the melee, falling backwards, and becoming a paraplegic after hitting the back of his neck on the corner of a wooden table. You also don't see the part where the guy who gets knocked-out cold by someone who was being aggressive with his wife, fails to make it home in time to tuck his kids in at night —he's too busy getting stitches in the emergency room. We don't see the heart attack that an older woman in the corner of the room is having caused by the sudden outbreak in violence. And we especially don't see the hundreds of thousands of dollars in lawsuits that often follow such caveman, primordial behavior.

Sex and Fights

What causes so many bar fights? Why aren't there nearly as many brawls at the supermarket, post office, or hardware store? We obviously know that alcohol plays a huge part in these barroom altercations, but there's a bit more to it than that. Alcohol is simply the catalyst that lights the match in the room full of explosives.

Two large men—complete strangers to one another—begin talking about the new power saw they simultaneously have their eyes on at their local Home Depot. The two dudes, through several minutes of grunting, scratching their nuts, and saying things like "hell yeah, brother," really bond over their same taste in saws.

They both decide to purchase one and pay at adjacent cashiers before exiting the store at the same time. One guy sees the other climb into his antique Ford Mustang.

"Love the ride, man! Can I check out what's under the hood?!"

"Sure, brother! Come check it out!"

The two gentleman yap about cars, tools, jobs, and some other stuff before shaking hands and parting ways. For a little under a half-hour, these two guys were practically best friends.

On another day at a different time, these same two guys are out drinking at the watering hole one evening. In this scenario we'll refer to the man with the Mustang as *Mark* and his admirer in automotive taste, *Pete*.

Upon arriving at the bar, Mark and his beautiful girlfriend, Sofia, pull up the only two unoccupied barstools in the room. After several shots and beers, Pete, who happens to be seated on the other side of Sofia, catches eyes with her after accidentally bumping her arm. "Pardon me," he says apologetically. "Don't worry about it," she says as she smiles back.

Mark eventually takes a trip to the restroom to drain the lizard, and when he gets back, he discovers that Sofia is now talking to this other guy. Her body positioning has changed, as she's now turned in a forty-five degree angle towards Pete. She's talking and laughing, and she neglects to acknowledge the return of Mark. The fact that this other guy who's talking to his girlfriend hasn't introduced himself yet draws Mark's ire.

Under sober circumstances, most people wouldn't think twice about this particular interaction, and in fact, upon returning from the john, Mark would have probably joined in on the conversation with friendly enthusiasm. People are generally social beings and we thrive off of communicative interaction. Maybe the world would be a better place if we struck-up conversation with complete strangers more often.

But Mark's *not* sober when he returns—he's a few shots and beers deep by now. He sips on his drink and watches the sports highlights on the TV, all while feeling ignored and keeping a keen ear to the conversation between his girlfriend and this stranger. The talk veers towards business, and as Sofia laughs uncontrollably at the other guy's witty comments, Mark sees him slip her his business card. As it turns out, Pete runs a marketing firm and has suggested to Sofia, who is trying to expand her privately-owned business, that his firm's services would be of great assistance.

When he sees this, Mark begins to beat his chest, so to speak.

"Yo! Did you just give my girl your number? You think I didn't see that? Who the fuck do you think you are?"

"Whoah! Calm down! I gave her my business card because she asked for it," Pete responds defensively and somewhat alarmed.

"Bullshit! I saw you eyeing her up!"

"Calm down, man. We were having an adult conversation. Relax."

That last teeny-weeny bit of condescending talk turns Mark into a growling, defensive knuckle-dragger intent on defending his territory.

Now, let's pause here for a minute. In relation to the prior example of the guys' interaction at Home Depot, how is the confessed admiration of Mark's shiny Mustang any different than Pete initiating conversation with Mark's girlfriend? Well, Mark wasn't drunk at the store. Pete simply thought that Mark's car was nice, and he wanted to communicate that. Both men had normal testosterone levels and a completely rational and contextualized interpretation of the interaction.

At the bar, on the other hand, Mark feels threatened by this smiling, friendly businessman. He's not worried about the business interests of his girlfriend, but instead that this man will be her choice of mate with whom to procreate. It sounds farfetched and dubious, but alcohol has a way of awakening the subconscious, often acting as the cataclysmic key that lets our primitive monster out of the basement.

Because of the unique way alcohol affects stress and instinct, each sip we take unveils more of the primal being inside of us that is clawing to get out. As it numbs our nerves it bolsters our emotions. When drunk, we laugh to the point of abdominal cramping, and we cry for just about no reason at all. We become paranoid, jealous, and angry about something that, in a sober state, probably wouldn't bother us. When we're sloshed, we hear the echoes of our genetic past. We become slobbering, stumbling, horny talking monkeys capable of doing very stupid and impulsive things.

Mark's primal identity slowly surfaces with each gulp of firewater. Although he may deny that he's fearful that his girlfriend will end up making babies with this marketing firm manager named Pete, it's exactly what the instinctual voices inside of him are yelling louder and louder. *He's challenging the survival of your bloodline! You must defend what is yours! Fight him! You're the alpha! Drive him away from the potential mother of your young!*

Had they been sober, the conversation amongst the three most likely would have been friendly, polite, and maybe even beneficial for their respective businesses. But they weren't sober. Mark couldn't drown-out the voice of his inner-ape, and consequentially, he challenged Pete—a challenge that he accepted as to not look weak in front of the others at the watering hole. It went to blows. Both were black and blue for days and earned themselves a spot on the wall of shame at the local bar, and were permanently banned. Oh—they spent lots of money on legal fees as well.

This kind of conflict isn't unique to men either. Women, as argued earlier, see other women as a threat to the procreation of their young as well. That's not to say that women consciously spend all day searching for the dong that will give her the baby of her dreams, but the thought *is* there. It's down in that dank basement area of the subconscious mind, and the door tends to come flying open after a bunch of tequila shots on an empty stomach.

Similarly to the paranoid, jealous, and insecure inner-ape of the male homo sapien, the instinctive urge of women is to do whatever's necessary to give birth to a healthy child. When a woman is scanning a guy's face, his abs, or his oiled-up biceps, she's internally judging his ability to provide the seed that will develop into a strong girl or boy. We've been programmed to want to sleep with those who will help our species move forward. The women who are perceived to birth the healthiest young and the men who appear to have the best chance of fighting off large predators or invading tribes are the most highly sought-after ones.

When piss-drunk, a woman will claw a bitch's face up if she believes that the other chick is trying to steal her man's seed. Just as it affects men, alcohol will amplify the jealous and survivalist being inside and will make a convincing case as to why she *should* take her high-heel off and beat that other slut to a bloody pulp with it.

From what I've seen behind the bar, ingrained sexual roles and desires can be powerful catalysts that, when combined with an excessive amount of booze, can result in some serious grudge matches. We like to think that we are civilized beings who are capable of carrying ourselves in a mature and reasonable manner. Granted, most people are capable of that under sober circumstances. But when you add alcohol to the mix, you're likely to see humans use the same conflict-resolution techniques that lions use on the African Plains.

Overcrowding

In today's world, there are simply too many of us packed into spaces that, frankly, are too small for us to not have the occasional freak-out.

Of all of the archetypal drinking establishments that bipedals like to frequent, crowded bars and nightclubs tend to host the most fisticuffs. If you've ever been squished so tightly into a subway car full of strangers to the point that you can't even scratch your ass, imagine if all of those people were hammered drunk—it would be an absolute bloodbath.

Think about all of the times you've tried to navigate a moving sea of cologne-soaked fist-pumpers with a drink in each hand, or when you were in a herd of thirsty bar visitors in hot pursuit of a cocktail from the bartender who's surrounded on all fronts. Elbows are thrown, toes are crunched, asscheeks are pinched, drinks are spilled, and threatening facial expressions are deployed when there are just too many drunken people in one area.

As beautiful and full of culture that big cities are, I would argue that we're not yet evolved or accustomed to living in such highly populated areas. Cramped living spaces and congested ways of travel can be very stressful for our brains that, for a *very* long time, were used to interacting with a small tribe or neighborhood. The more people that there are in one confined space, the more stress we are likely to endure. And in terms of conflict at the watering hole, high stress levels + high BAC levels = conflict.

A Bloody New Year's Eve

I was behind the stick at the Italian bar on New Year's Eve—a night infamous for wild behavior and drama. There was a very diverse collection of guests that evening, ranging from elderly Italian folk out for a nice New Year's meal, to young, sexy-as-all-hell girls sporting fishnet stockings, corsets, and stilettos. Bottle service was offered to those who wanted to spend way too much money on approximately twenty-five ounces of liquor. The DJ got the party going early, and its exploding momentum drove it to heights uncontainable.

As the dinner rush came to an end, the bartenders decided that we were all going to indulge in some champagne. I was operating on an empty stomach, so the bubbly resulted in me feeling pretty buzzed, pretty quickly. Once I started to feel silly, I failed to see the royal rumble that was brewing in opposite corners of the restaurant. There was always a Mafioso feel to this place. Gangster movies regularly played on the 160-inch projector screen above the bar. Certain guests always looked around the room before they, under their breath, mentioned "the family" or "the business." There was rarely a shortage of what appeared to be prostitutes accompanying management during business meetings in the basement. Oh, and there was usually a cloud of white powder that seemed to float in the night air.

The frequenters and the shenanigans only became increasingly sketchier as the hour hand moved further and further clockwise. It was a place that attracted those who wanted to show off what they had: clothes, money, women, spray tans, and in this particular case—weapons.

I began to notice that the two separate groups of men started to flock closer to each other. And every time the distance shrunk between them, it became more and more obvious to us that they weren't exactly cronies. Already hammered-drunk, they were beginning to talk shit amongst themselves—about the other pack of men—at a volume just loud enough for the others to catch wind. Their cocktail tables were now their proverbial campfires as they boosted each other's egos and prepared to do battle.

I didn't see it happen—I heard it. A few seconds earlier, one of the other bartenders saw a guy go into the men's room followed by two dudes from the other pack. It wasn't long after that when I heard lots of crashing, yelling, and cursing. A fight had broken out between the three men, and once the rest of the two groups realized it, the benches cleared and the gloves came off. All of the employees still working at the time of the melee all looked at each other with the same expression—*uh oh*—and began to try and stop it. Any attempt seemed futile as we realized that we had let this thing get out of control. There were several large combatants throwing rights and lefts, swinging bottles, and bleeding everywhere.

What's a bartender to do when such a conflict occurs? Do you stand idly by and allow your bar to be ripped apart by warring knuckle draggers? Of course not! You put down the martini shaker, make sure your shoes are tied, secure any loose clothing that could be used to strangle you or hold you down, and go after the worst tipper of the bunch! I suggest using either a bottle of Galliano or Belvedere as these are typically the heaviest bottles behind the average bar that one could use to clock someone with.

Like a line change during a hockey game, we jumped over the bar and onto the field of battle. Along with our coked-up owner, Danny, our bouncer, and yours truly began to force our way into the pack of fighting men, trying to promote peace and understanding, *mannn*. We yelled and pleaded for them to break it up, but as you could probably imagine, they didn't.

We were now in the middle of it all, getting slammed into like in a mosh pit at a heavy metal show. When I finally received an errant overhand right to the side of my head, time slowed down. For an instant, all I could see were English soldiers trying to whoop my fellow Scotsman. I was now in the movie *Braveheart*, and Mel Gibson told me to fight, and so I did—sorta.

I quickly succumbed to my own rage and grabbed the guy whose fist had just connected with my face only seconds prior. I shoved him into the wall, and when he bounced back towards me, I neutralized him. Fifteen-ish years spent training in martial arts, wrestling, and grappling helped me subdue him with ease. I got double-underhooks under his armpits, placed my right leg behind his right leg, and swept him to the ground with an impromptu judo hip toss. On the ground is where I kept him until something more alarming drew my attention.

Weapons were now about to be introduced to this debacle. I heard glass break and became very worried when I saw one of the grunting, bloodthirsty combatants wielding a half-shattered, jagged bottle of Stolichnaya vodka in his hand. This slug fest was about to get extra bloody.

More and more guys began throwing punches over top of others. Those who lay limp on the floor were kicked repeatedly while they were down and out. Bodies were dropping to the floor as if they were running on electricity and the power was abruptly cut. As I finally let my squirming wrestling partner free, I began to assist in the process of at least trying to push everyone outside. By doing that, we could at least pour *some* baking soda on this rapidly intensifying flame.

Usually, when a fight or argument is pushed out into the parking lot, there tends to be a collective sigh of relief from all of the employees involved in the attempt to break it up. They become someone else's problem at that point. But on this night, we desperately tried to reverse the traffic of shuffling feet that were imprinting bloody footprints on the way out. *EVERYONE BACK INSIDE! NOW!*

When I saw an elongated magazine protruding from a machine gun, I dove for cover and bear-crawled back into the main foyer. I was expecting to hear rounds being discharged at any second. My squinting eyes and clenched teeth prepared me to feel the fragments of brick and sheetrock that made up our walls showering me as I tried to escape the spray of bullets. Luckily, it never came to that.

I made it into the kitchen and was connected to a 911 dispatcher after making a mayday call. "Units have already been dispatched," the female voice calmly said. I hung up immediately and listened for voices from the main dining room. By now, the groups were separated—one outside and one inside. I decided that if this guy with the hand-cannon decides to come inside and follow through on his threats, I was not going to be associated with these ass-clowns who were *still* talking shit, and be shot dead where I stood. I ran through the restaurant to the back exit where I peered out through the door. The police already had the guy spread-eagle on the pavement and were placing him in handcuffs.

The drunkards in the foyer acted like nothing happened despite looking like they had just made their way through a meat grinder. Blood and broken glass covered the floor. The group of men—barely standing—heckled their adversaries who were being wrestled and corralled by the police. They shouted insults and war-cries until more police arrived and eventually arrested them, too.

Danny and I felt that we deserved at least a beer for our peacekeeping efforts, so we walked through the rubble back to the bar, cracked open a cold one, and toasted to each other. We hadn't suffered any significant damage ourselves, but the bar was in pretty bad shape. We both realized that we had barely escaped a potential massacre.

Why Can't We Be Friends?

In a perfect world, we would all go to the same party and have a great time together. We would buy each other drinks, tip our hats to the person next to us, hold the door for each other—even wipe the toilet seat dry of the piss we soaked it with. But let's face it—we're far from perfect. Yeah, there are many amazing people out there, but the fact remains that many of us are assholes. Alcohol just makes it worse.

Bar fights seem to be a part of our culture and sadly don't seem to be disappearing anytime soon. Romantic ideas of barroom combat and the instinctive competitive spirit we embody as human beings are both catalysts that spark conflict at the watering hole. But make no mistake—alcohol is the whopper of catalysts. As much fun as alcohol really is to guzzle, it has a way of turning us into unpredictable animals.

Will there ever be peace at the watering hole? Only time will tell, I guess. Although the human mind is incredibly complex, in many ways, we still operate according to the same system of genetic predisposition and instinct that our ancient ancestors operated by—*especially* when we're blitzed.

After a few stiff drinks, our inhibitions fall by the wayside, and in their place appear the deepest emotions and desires from our subconscious mind. Ernest Hemmingway once said "Write drunk; edit sober." He seemed to do his best writing after a few choice alcoholic beverages, when he had no filter. He bled onto the page and cleaned it up in the morning...or whenever he eventually sobered-up.

The filter that prevents the literary "bleeding" that Hemmingway alluded to is the same filter that would normally help us regulate our paranoid, jealous, and/or hostile drunken thoughts. When we're three sheets to the wind, we speak our minds more freely than usual. In a bar full of intoxicated people, each word or action that slips past our weakening filters has the potential to be the flaming match that ends up igniting the whole room in conflict.

10
Gratuity

Naturally, I was quite thirsty after tirelessly roaming the confines of the local watering hole during this project. I became dangerously dehydrated after avoiding the constant onslaught of solicitations to mate from that dreaded 'Deloris' creature, and so I approached one of the bartenders for a frothy beverage.

I handed him a piece of local currency—a coin that was given to me by a popular frequenter named Wild Bill that entitled me to one drink. The hospitable bartender poured a beer for me, and I quickly thanked him, took a sip, and turned away thinking nothing more of it.

Strangely,I felt something hit my back when I walked away. It made me jump and swat at the air, as I had a brief flashback of getting attacked by killer bees while on safari two years back. I breathed a sigh of relief as I saw that there were no bees, but rather the very same coin I handed to the bartender for my beer laying right at my feet. I was puzzled, but I needed to get back to my notepad. The show had to go on.

When I approached the bar once more about an hour later, I exchanged my own currency this time—a few quarter-dollar coins I found in my trousers—for another frothy beverage. I made sure that the bartender accepted my payment, because I had assumed that it had somehow slipped out of his hands and accidentally hit me in the back during our last transaction. I told him to make sure that he kept this payment safe.

Wham! Immediately when I turned around to head back towards my notepad, I was struck in the back again! At that point, I thought that maybe it was a local custom resembling some form of gratitude for my purchase—a strange one, if so. But in my experience, some of the indigenous people I've bumped into during my career as a zoologist had some extremely bizarre customs. "You're welcome," I shouted back at him. I assumed my position in the corner of the room to continue with my observations.

The sun had set a bit further now, and the population density of the natives increased greatly since my last trip to see the bartender. I wanted another drink, so I tried to delicately maneuver myself amongst them towards the bar so to not disrupt their natural behavior. As I snaked my way to about a meter's distance from the bar top, I tried to get the bartender's attention. I waved and shouted his title 'bartender' over and over again. Nothing was working, and I was getting very thirsty.

From my time spent in the wild, I know how important eye contact can be. I've relied on a stern stare into the eyes of a man-eating beast several times during my career in order to save my own life. At other times, it was important to avoid eye contact as to not anger the animal I was observing and interacting with. On this occasion, however, I decided it was my best bet to open my eyes wide and stare the bartender down in an attempt to gain his attention.

Unfortunately, my glare seemed to anger him. He barked at me as if he was a baboon protecting his young from an intruder. I doubt that he became aggressive with me simply because I looked him in the eyes for a few seconds. I don't know what I did to piss 'em off so much, but I became worried as I knew that if I didn't get a drink soon, I'd have to resort to sipping from Deloris' lipstick-stained glass. I would rather swap saliva with a dog who eats his own shit...

***

Willy was hit in the back by those coins because he didn't tip. The bartender couldn't help but display his displeasure at not receiving a tip for his services. This pissed-off reaction will be later highlighted in chapter 12—"The Bitch Fest." But for now, let's start at the ground level.

What is tipping? It's is a strange concept if you really examine it. It's a fairly new word in terms of its etymology, which after much investigation via Google search and some dusty old linguistic books, still leaves me scratching my head a bit. It is, in all reality, giving charity to those who aren't exactly doing charitable work, isn't it? Well, not exactly.

The Oxford English Dictionary states that the word "tip" (in monetary terms—not male reproductive anatomy slang, you sicko) began to surface in the 1700s. Some say that the word "tip" evolved as an acronym which stood for *"to i(e)nsure proper service"* or *"to i(e)nsure promptitude"* in many of the service establishments across Great Britain.

One theory of the evolution of tipping as we know it today—primarily that which takes place in restaurants and bars—suggests that gratuity was trending in the days of the wild west, in outlaw-occupied towns with one long and centralized street, a few stores and barns for travelers to rest their overworked horses, and a bar or two. This was a period of vast expansion and pioneering into the unknown that saw many a man travel west in search of riches, to escape the law, or perhaps flee from an angry wife.

Dirty, tired, hungry, and thirsty, these travelers—many times humping it alone—would stumble into the town saloon looking for a drink and possibly some information. Upon kicking open the swinging doors, he would trudge up to the bartender, and ask for bourbon, a beer, and a meal. After doing so, he would leave a small amount of money—separate from the price of the meal—on the bar top for the bartender, who in that particular ecosystem, was not *just* a bartender.

It was thought that bartenders had an extensive knowledge of the goings on about the town. They were usually familiar with everything and everyone. If you were a lone rambler in the days prior to smartphones and tourist welcome centers in search of information, it would have behooved you to take care of the man pouring your drinks. If not, he might be inclined to serve you a bowl of his 14 year-old bloodhound's doggie chow instead of the chili that you ordered. It's important to note that there isn't exactly much literature on this theory, but I think it's the sexiest one.

Non-Negotiable

This hyphenated term is what many restaurant and bar employees see stamped across the paychecks that they receive every two weeks or so, accompanied by the numerical representation of income earned—a big fat "$0."

In fact, most servers and bartenders across the United States are paid a whopping $2.13 per hour—that's half of what minimum wage was in 1991. There are exceptions in several states, including California where service industry employees are paid upwards of $9 per hour. But generally, most make nothing from hourly pay or salary. There have been several raises of the federal minimum wage since then, but the majority of tipped restaurant and bar employees have been left behind because to certain exemptions. This is due to the government's acknowledgment of the expectation of being tipped—even the government expects a patron to take care of his or her bartender/server.

This is the primary reason why tipped restaurant employees get so cranky after a bad tip. The tip isn't an extra. It's not a pat on the back for going above and beyond, nor is it exclusive to people who have a lot of cash to throw around. Gratuity, in fact, should be considered a requirement. In the restaurant industry of the United States, it's a socially agreed upon payment for services rendered by a server or bartender.

On occasion, a strung-out server or bartender curses out a guest, is lazy and doesn't perform their job according to reasonable expectations, or is simply just a cunt of a human being; in which case, yeah, you could argue that they don't deserve a tip. I'd agree with that.

But for the sake of argument, if you receive service that is anything above shitty, you are socially obligated to leave a tip on top of the cost of your meal and/or beverage. Otherwise, you are stealing and will be smitten by Ninkasi.

A tip shouldn't be something to get the calculator out for. Stop it—you're embarrassing yourself. To leave twenty-percent on a double-digit check, simply take the tens place holder and double it. For example, if your tab comes to $40, a twenty-percent tip would be $8. To leave a fifteen-percent tip, just shave a little bit off of the twenty-percent number. Don't freak out about it.

Tips come in all forms and sizes in the service industry. Some are miniscule and insulting, some are right where they should be, some are gigantic and unexpected, and others— well, sometimes they're...not usable money. I've been given Japanese currency, two-dollar bills (I know they're technically usable, but honestly—who pays for anything with a two-dollar-bill?), rolls of quarters, hotel room keys, and nudity. Yeah, I like seeing some sexy girl's rack just like the rest of em,' but darling—I can't do anything with that except rub my face in it. I'd rather have real-life currency. If I want to rub my face in someone's rack, I'll take the money you leave as a tip and spend it at the strip club after work.

The Rat Pack

As is quite characteristic of an upscale Italian restaurant in the northeast, a few goombahs strutted in during the later hours of the evening reeking of cigar smoke and cologne, looking for a spot at the bar to put down a few. For anyone who has seen the movie *Goodfellas*, a pack of well-dressed Italian men is a very welcome sight for anyone in the hospitality industry, *especially* if they're accompanied by women. They tip well, and they tip often.

They tip you as they barge into your personal space and greet you with a kiss on the cheek and a hand clenched around the back of your neck. They tip you as you pour them snifters of Campari, and as you plead for the chef to make them their special *gabagool* that isn't offered on the regular menu.

They'll tip you as you stand there just picking your wedgie.

On this particular night, six or seven Joe Pescis and Robert Deniros joined me at the watering hole, all high on triumph and blow as they were celebrating some sort of business buyout, or as the short one with the squeaky voice put it, "puttin' them rat bastahds out on the fuckin' streets!" Dom Perignon would be the preferred juice for this particular victory lap—a bottle that costed them just shy of $400 each.

The funny thing was that these guys barely drank a sip (that doesn't go to say that they weren't on constant parade to the restroom to do lines of coke), yet they continued to tip me. I guess it was their way of compensating me for intentionally putting me in extremely uncomfortable situations that night.

I was asked questions like "So, Jack, how much would you pay to fuck my girl?"

They purposefully mispronounced my name seemingly to further establish their alpha status over me.

"How much do you think her tits ran me?"

Um...honestly? Not that much. They look like two plastic bags of smashed ass.

"C'mon, you wanna' fuck my girl, don't ya? Tell her, Jack. Take her in the bathroom, do a line off of those tits, and fuck her right in the ass."

I could, but am *not* making this shit up. I assure you.

"What, she isn't good enough for you?"

Now, being that I was about twenty-three years old with barely a whisker on my face and minimal experience in the bar business, it goes without saying that I felt a little out of my element. Yet, I remained sturdy and steadfast and responded back with enough smart-ass answers and comebacks to keep them entertained. As we bickered back and forth, I rose to the occasion, meeting what seemed to be their requirements of gaining their respect...and gratuity.

I continued to pour expensive champagne and awkwardly dodge solicitations to bang this guy's doped-up girl in the restroom. As they paid their tab, which by now had amounted to over $900 in a matter of a few hours, the head goombah wrapped his arm around the back of my neck and pulled me in close. His garlicky breath infiltrated my nose as he whispered "You know Jack...you're OK." Then he dumped another ball of cash on the bar, and led the celebration towards the exit.

The drunken and generous group of guys and gals were high on life—and booze and yayo—as they all left the bar, but not before the squeaky guy demanded that his chick lift up her cocktail dress for me. "Show Jack your pussy. C'mon! Do it!"

He laughed hysterically at his own pun: "Don't be a pussy—show em' your pussayyyy!"

Without hesitation, she did as she was told, and as I got a full-frontal view of what lay beneath, let's just say I was thankful that I didn't take him up on his earlier solicitation.

"What do ya' think of that, eh Jack? Last chance," he giggled as he gave me the middle-finger and hopped out of the room. "Fine, ya faggot. Have a good night!"

And me? As they danced out the front door singing Dean Martin, I took a deep breath. The night was done and I could now let my guard down. When it was all said and done, they had left me over $600.00 in tips in less than two hours.

Coaster Throws

The flashy goombah with the thick wad of money and little regard for what happens to it is not a rare phenomenon at any establishment—especially in New Jersey—that advertises itself with the words "Vino e Cucina," and where the tunes of Frank Sinatra and Dean-O belt over the speakers on a regular basis. These charismatic, high-rollin' ballers are *not*, however, a common sight at an Irish Pub. Enter Erik.

Erik is a man I met only once—a stout man of normal height and could have even been classified as a bit stocky. He was dressed exquisitely, as was the entourage that followed him in on this particular night. His goatee, black with small patches of gray, made him look even more paramount. "A man you don't want to cross," is how one of his crew described him later on. Although I had seen my fair share of wannabe mobsters while working at the pretender's club down the road, I believed what I had been told. Erik did not seem like a pretender.

On a very laggard and dreary Tuesday night, Danny and I had decided that we were going to close-up shop a bit early and escape back to his place for some Magners cider on draft, compliments of his often lifesaving kegerator. Just as we began cleaning, Erik and his wolf pack came strutting through the doors for what appeared to be one last drink to top-off their adventures for the evening. This took the wind right out of our sails immediately.

There is just something incredibly annoying and troublesome about dealing with late-night boozers when you've already decided to start closing. But what do you do? Do you turn them away to the road from which they came? Do you expel them like stray puppies looking for a meal or a puddle to sip from, just to be able to cut your losses and flee from work early to catch last call somewhere else? Not on this night. We reluctantly placed a few of our newly-delivered coasters down on the bar and began to greet them and take drink requests.

After placing several Kettle One and tonics and a few glasses of wine on the bar, I asked their *Don*—Erik—if he would like to start a tab. When he said yes while simultaneously handing me a fifty dollar bill, I became confused.

"So, you don't want me to start you a tab?" I asked, unsure of his intentions.

"No, start me a tab," he replied in a scratchy voice as if he had spent all night smoking cigars, gargling scotch, and howling at the moon.

"Well, you want me to cash this out and *then* start you a tab?" I asked while waving the fifty in the air. I obviously didn't want this guy to think I was jipping him or anything.

"No, put that in the tip jar and start me a tab."

When I turned to look at Danny, just to see if he was catching all of this, he looked back at me with a wide-eyed, raised eyebrow look of surprise. I hesitated, and when I did, Erik barked at me until I gently placed the fifty-dollar bill into the tip jar. No matter how many times it happens, someone giving me money that I feel that I really haven't earned is an uncomfortable occurrence. It's kind of like getting a Christmas card full of money from your beloved grandmother that you know needs it more than you do. Erik, however, did not need that fifty. Nor did he need the several fifties and hundreds that followed.

Boredom, restlessness, the desire to project power—or all three, perhaps, prompted Erik to ask for an unopened pack of drink coasters. It wasn't a big deal. Hell, we get them for free from alcohol reps and distributors, so we really didn't care. It's always cute when a guest shyly asks if it would be OK for them to take a coaster home with them. *I dunno, I could get in a lot of trouble, but since you've treated me to such nice cleavage during the course of the night, I'll make an exception.*

So why then, when I handed him a pack, did he place a crisp Benjamin in my hand? Because it was chump change and he didn't really give a shit, I guess. Most likely, however, it was to pay in advance for the mess that he was about to make.

The bar top and floor were soon covered with drink coasters. Danny and I were dodging the flying cardboard squares like Keanu Reeves had dodged bullets in *The Matrix*. He was flinging these things all over the place, and had apparently made a game of trying to send them hurling through our expensive array of bourbon and whiskey bottles to the other side of the room. And on the other side of the room, mind you, were several other stragglers that had muddled into the pub looking for a nightcap.

As Danny handed Erik a fresh pack to reload his coaster quiver in exchange for yet another fifty-dollar bill, I was explaining to the guests on the other side of the whiskey case that they had better keep their heads down and eyes protected. As Danny and I exchanged glances of disbelief, Erik continued to unleash volley after volley of flying coasters and simultaneously make it rain into our tip jar. He was like a kid in a candy shop with a lot more means to acquire candy than the other kids.

After a few more cocktails and thousands of drink coasters later, Erik did something that left me speechless. I did not expect this alpha male—this emperor of his kind—to grab my hand and kiss it as if *I* was royalty. That's right, after our 50th handshake of the evening, he grabbed my right hand, yanked it to him with the same aggressiveness and velocity as that famous panda bear who mauled some guy through the zoo fence and robbed him of his jacket, and planted a big wet one firmly on the topside of my paw.

I was flabbergasted—absolutely bamboozled by this guy's schizophrenic behavior. He now bowed to *me*! He had just payed homage to his court jester. After taking care of his tab (that he paid for without even looking at the total amount), he pulled me in close, clenched the back of my neck like a Muy Thai fighter clinching his opponent, and thanked me for a wonderful evening. Just like that, they were gone.

"What the fuck just happened?" Danny asked aloud—partly to me, but mostly to himself.

Oh the carnage! When the group of ultimate-coaster players and the lingering last call folk disappeared into the night, we sat back and tried to catch our breath and realize what exactly had just taken place.

I felt like Tom Hanks' character in the classic *Saving Private Ryan*, Captain Miller, in a confused daze after enduring the hectic invasion of Omaha Beach. I was mesmerized and hypnotized by the devastation that was the pub that evening. We knew we were in for a long night of cleaning, but we also knew that we had just made a killing on a night where we should have gone home practically penniless.

Normally, we never touched the tip jars or the cash drawers until all of the cleaning and stocking of booze was complete, but on this night we were like two little kids that couldn't wait for Christmas morning to open their presents. We overturned the tip jar and watched the fifties and hundreds gently float through the air down to the bar top. A few bills more, and we could have swam the backstroke through the mound of money that lay before us.

Erik had just made a huge contribution to my retirement fund.

The above were obviously stories of fabulous gratuity and generosity—circumstances that tend to be few and far between in the lives of most bartenders—me included. Whether by luck, hard work, or a combination of both, I have received some incredibly lavish tips during my tenure as a drink slinger. Greeny and I were once tipped $1,000 after we threw a private party while dressed in coconut bras, grass skirts, and mullets. Total working time was about six hours. But as with most things in life, there is a balance—a yin and a yang to everything. Sometimes, the tips we get as bartenders are so awful—so insulting—that we have to act. And we do. And we will. We're crazy like that, yo.

Dippin' Dicks

There are checks and balances at work in our universe. Where there is big, there is small. Where there's good, there's evil, and where there is generous, there is cheap. These natural parallels work to keep us honest and constantly evolving as a species, and to remind us that nothing is to be taken for granted.

For some reason, I notice the cheap more than the generous. I don't know why that is, exactly, but I would imagine it has to do with the same reason why people sit on their couches glued to Fox News and all of their fear mongering. If it's bad, we humans want to know about it. Good news doesn't sell advertising as well as bad news.

The bar guest who leaves a five-percent tip tends to linger on my mind long after the cute couple who left a $20 tip on a $30 check does. Why is that? Do we remember those who trespass against us more than those who do good by us?

We complex, yet highly predictable talking monkeys are likely to remember the one asswipe who cut us off in traffic more than the twenty or so people who let us merge in front of them earlier on in our commute. In the ecosystem of the watering hole, bartenders *never* forget a shitty tipper. You'll get attention alright. And maybe you'll even get *some* service, but karma—sometimes taking the form of a penis—

will surely be coming to pay you or your drink a visit sooner or later.

If you remember earlier on during Danny's introduction and the tidbit about the carefree clobbering of that boat captain with a bait fish, you might draw the conclusion that Danny doesn't like to be taken advantage of. As generous, giving, and thoughtful as Danny may be, when you take liberties against him, he *will* find a way to restore balance to the *penisdulum* of justice. See what I did there?

While slinging drinks behind the bar at a busy nightclub, you're bound to encounter more than a fair share of tools and bitches. There's no shortage of pretentious, materialistic, and egotistical douchebags at a joint where it costs $30 just to enter a room—and that's *after* everyone stands in the line that extends down the street and around the corner, shivering in the cold or melting in the humidity.

There was a special event taking place on this particular evening, and each guest was given two tickets that they were to give to the bartender in exchange for a beverage paid for by the hosts of the occasion. This is common practice for large networking gatherings or celebrations such as a film release or retirement.

At this moment in time, Danny was six or so people deep with the DJ spinning house music at full-throttle, and as one could probably imagine, that didn't leave him with much ability to make small talk.

"Yo! Boss! Yo! Bartender! Lemme get a Patron!"

Danny had been ignoring this self-serving boob's yelping for a good while now, but with a small break in the action, he finally paid him the attention that the guy was craving so desperately. With stern eye contact and a nod of the head, Danny acknowledged him and started making his drink.

He had asked for a single shot of Patron with a wedge of lime. Danny was sure of it. But when he presented it to the guy in exchange for a drink ticket, it was pushed back towards him.

"Nah, yo. I wanted it on the rocks. I thought you heard me."

No you didn't, you twat.

"My bad," responded Danny in the most unapologetic of tones. He then took the shot, poured it into a rocks glass over ice, and gave the guy his drink. "Got that ticket for me?"

"Oh shit. I think I left my tickets at the welcome table. I'll be right back, bro." Not surprisingly, he didn't return to keep his end of the deal. He didn't leave a tip, either. *Roger that*, Danny thought, mentally signing the guy's death warrant.

If you go to an event where everything is paid for, such as a wedding or some other kind of banquet, you should spare yourself the embarrassment of being looked at as a slimy piece of shit and tip the service personnel. They're not your servants. They work for the guy or gal who paid for you to be there. Conjure up what little dignity you have and leave a fucking dollar. You don't get ahead in life by being a stingy tightwad.

The night continued fairly smoothly for the bar staff as most of the guests exchanged their remaining tickets for drinks and left decent tips. It was proving to be a fun night, yet Dan the man couldn't rid the annoyance that the poorly-mannered Patron drinker stirred in him. And soon enough, he came back for more.

"Yo! Boss! Hey buddy! Bartender!"

At this point, Danny was serving people to the guy's left, right, and those behind him. He was working around him to prove a point. As each guest received their drink, they placed a dollar or two on the bar as a tip. Danny slowly and methodically collected each tip, raised them in the air and floated them like kites past the face of the shouting grease ball, who at this point, was becoming even more impatient and annoyed.

See that? You tip me—you get a drink! See how this works?

The demonstration backfired.

When the adjacent guests were taken care of first, our man of mystery was finally acknowledged, and when he was, he demanded four drinks of the same kind. Each guest was only given two tickets for this event, so there was no way that he was going to let him get away with being a cheap prick this time. If he wanted four, he'd have to pay for three, being that Danny already let him off the hook with the first one. It was a fairly formal event thrown by some pretty powerful people—he didn't think he'd have to shake anyone down for a few bucks to cover a small drink tab.

"On the rocks, right?"

"Yeah. Four of em'."

"I'm going to need to see your tickets first, sir. You still owe me from last time."

Quite surprised, Danny sees this guy throw his tickets down on the bar as if he was laying down four Aces during a poker game. He had obviously gotten them from someone else at the party. The friend he was with helped him with the drinks as they carried them off through the sea of guests and out of sight, failing once again to leave a tip. This time, his fellow drink slingers were eye witnesses.

That's it! It's on like Donkey Kong!

A good while passed with the music still thumping and the drinks still flowing. The bartenders were having a great time —including our protagonist. Yet he was unable to rid his mind of revengeful thoughts. He hates to lose. And at that moment, he felt like he was losing.

But as luck would have it, the yipping hyena returned, determined to get service. The crowd at the bar was still three or four people deep, and the bartenders were still cranking. As he made the slightest of eye contact with his thirsty adversary, his blood began to boil. Adrenaline was now flowing through his veins and his hair stood on end. Danny was preparing to strike.

"Yo! Bartender! Bartender! Yo! Buddy!"

This time, Danny went straight to the source. Instead of making him wait, our valiant and virtuous vindicator approached the villain with great vigor and stared through his eyes and into his empty soul.

"What can I do for you, sir?"

"Yo! You heard me this time," he declared with chuckle and a goofy smile, his glazed-over eyes revealing his intoxicated state. "Yo, hook me up with four more."

After acknowledging his request, Danny made it a point to get the attention of the rest of his crew. He wanted all eyes on him as he was about to swing for the fences. He poured the four drinks and placed them on the bar—two in front, and two in the rear.

"Got my tickets?"

"Nah, yo. I talked to the manager though. He said it was fine. I'm boys with the guys who are in charge of this thing."

Wrong. He continued his plea bargain.

"Yo, I'll be right back for the other two. Just don't let anyone put anything in em'," he said jokingly. The problem was that no one was laughing. He just left his newborn calf with a pack of hungry predators.

Like a jaguar waiting in the high grass patiently stalking its prey with the highest degree of resolve and focus, Danny took his shot. He had been performing reconnaissance on the enemy since his first offense, and made the distinction that he was alone this time. He had no help to carry the drinks away.

Bartender intuition would have our champion assume that the first two drinks were probably hand-delivered by our self-inflated and aloof challenger. He seemed like a guy pathetically trying to impress the right people, and if this proved to be true, he probably would have passed the first two drinks off to those whom he was brown-nosing that night. This meant that one of the cocktails still left on the bar would be consumed by the enemy. Now was the time to act.

Poison? Spit? Chards of glass? Droplets of Visine, perhaps? Oh! I know…Penis!

Channeling the quick-striking prowess of a boa constrictor, Danny snatched one of the remaining two cocktails off of the bar. He held them out of visible range, unbuckled his belt, pulled out a boa constrictor of his own, and submerged it into the ice-cold glass of premium tequila blanco. He closed his eyes and enjoyed the sweet sensation (and constriction) of revenge.

His fellow drink slingers watched in awe while trying to not make it too obvious that they were all staring at Danny swishing his dick around in someone's drink—an offense that would probably get them all fired and worse. But they couldn't help but laugh under their breath at what Danny had executed. They were laughing, but probably not very surprised. They were witnessing a beautiful act of rebellion, a flawless symphony of retribution.

Once he had his way with the first drink, he put it back up on the bar and sacked the second. Again, he lowered it to where no one could see it, and proceeded to prison rape this beverage that had a 50/50 chance of touching the lips and mouth of his target. When he was finally finished, he scooped a few ice cubes back into the drink to replace the ones he had forced out with his cock-and-balls. Below the bar surface, it was utter chaos—a violation of epic proportions. Above the bar surface, however, Danny never broke character.

As this unaware butthead returned for his cocktail garnished with karma and pubic hair, Danny gently budged the two glasses towards him.

"Thank you, sir. Hope you have a great night."

A half-assed nod was all that he got in return, and as predicted, no tip was put on on the bar—only in his drink.

That night's game ended as such: Danny – 1. Cheap, obnoxious, scrotum-sweat sucker—0.

Why We Tip

Tipping in a bar is very important. Like mentioned before, most bartenders are paid so minimally that they regularly receive paychecks worth absolutely nothing. Their hourly pay is just enough to cover basic law and tax practice, so when you don't tip your bartender, you are fucking them. I actually would make the case that it's a form of thievery.

Now, why should you have to pay another dollar on top of a Guinness that already costed you six bucks? I mean, all the bartender really did, in theory, was open a valve so that beer could flow into a glass, hand it to you, and then take your money, right? Does that *really* warrant being tipped? The answer is a most definite *YES!*

At the most basic level, you tip your bartender just for being there. Think about it: if you don't tip the guy or gal pouring your drinks, and the house doesn't pay them either, that means they are working for free. Who likes working for free? Nuns, I guess. But aside from them—not many people really enjoy it at all, in fact.

Those who pour your drinks need to pay the bills just like everyone else, and when their shift ends with an empty paycheck and an empty tip jar, you can bet that they'll find employment elsewhere. In order to keep staff on board to continue to serve you their product, the house would have to pay their service staff either hourly, or with a salary.

177

Guess what folks, simple business theory tells us that in order to cover their employees' pay, they would have to raise the cost of their product. That means that your Guinness would cost maybe one, even two extra dollars! Do you see what is trending here?

No matter what, if you want a refuge at which to drown your sorrows, an escape from Mom and Dad's house to meet up with that hottie you just met, or just a place to sip on some beers and watch the game, you *will* pay one way or another. Why not take care of the person who is *directly* taking care of you?

Don't be cheap, folks. I sincerely mean it when you don't have to shower us with Benjamins like Erik did. We surely won't stop you, though. And you can bet that if you do spoil us, your wait time to get a drink on that busy night at the club will be at zero minutes. But a simple dollar on a drink, or a fifteen to 20-percent sign of gratuity is greatly appreciated, and in my opinion, usually deserved.

We *Tip* in 'Merica!

I was behind the stick one night at the Irish pub when about thirty young folk came in to celebrate the 21st birthday of one of their friends. They seemed nice and pleasant, and so I was nice and pleasant. I am usually very honest when it comes to giving a rating to my own execution of service. And on this night, on a scale of one-to-ten, I was working somewhere in-between an eight and a nine.

When I started serving-up their first round of drinks—most of which were fruity cocktails for the ladies and hipster drinks like an old-fashioned or a sazerac for the gentlemen, I began to notice an alarming trend. After being asked if they'd like to start a tab, they declined and said that most of them would be paying with cash. The red flag was raised when I didn't see any currency left over on the bar afterwards.

They're young kids. They will probably tip on the next round.

That ended up being a false hope. I made another twenty drinks or so, and as I took payment for each individual one, I noticed that the only paper that lay on my bar were napkins folded and squished around a piece of chewed bubblegum.

They probably just aren't aware of the custom of leaving tips with each round when you pay with cash.

It was when I started making the third round of drinks that my hospitable smile shriveled into a hostile, anger-clenching puckered expression of loathing, hatred, and murderous thoughts. Some of the guests at the party were beginning to put their coats on. It looked like they were getting ready to head to the next stop on their bargain-basement barcrawl. It was now time to act. I grabbed the microphone to the house speaker system, climbed up onto my soapbox, and prepared my hate speech.

"Just a question, guys," my voice echoed through the room. "How many of you are from Europe?"

I'd say about half of the room (at this point it was just their group remaining) looked up and then over at me. The other half continued being their cheap-fuck selves.

"No Europeans here, eh? That's interesting. You see, in Europe, it's not really customary to tip your bartender that much, if at all. I figured that, because I have yet to receive

179

any compensation for my services thus far this evening, maybe we had some Norwegians or Frenchies in the crowd. Oui? Oui? No."

The whole room was now tuned-in. The music was off, their mouths were shut, and it was only my vengeful voice that sounded throughout the bar.

"By a show of hands, guys, who likes to work for free? Anyone? No one. Hmm, that's what I figured. Yeah, we do have that in common. I definitely don't like to work for free either. But that's what I'm doing right now, guys. For the past hour and a half, I've been providing you a service that I have yet to be compensated for."

As I heard a chick in the crowd scoff at me in disbelief and disgust, I barked back. I felt like Adam Sandler's Character in *The Wedding Singer*. I didn't care if they were interested in what I had to say or not. I had the microphone and they didn't, so they were going to listen to each and every word I had to say.

"Guess what! If I don't make tip-y, I no work-y. If I—and I speak for *all* bartenders—don't work, then you don't have a place to hang out other than the parking lot at Wendy's or your Mom and Dad's basement. So for the rest of the time you're here, whether that's until last call, or for only 5 minutes more, I will not serve another drink until I see some dollar bills on the bar!"

How's that for non-negotiable?!

(In my best leprechaun impression:) *I couldn't believe me eyes!* They lined-up like penguins waiting to approach the edge of the iceberg, or like a somber crowd at a viewing

180

waiting to pay their respects. Aside from a mound of dollar bills on the bar, they delivered to me their apologies and half-assed excuses such as "I'm sorry bro, I usually leave a tip at the end." No you don't. Not with cash you dunce. Not when you don't have a tab running.

As I began to cool off, I told them that I had just taught them a valuable life lesson and armed them with knowledge of how to have a nice night out without crossing an angry troll of a bouncer toss you into the dumpster in the back alley.

11
Ethics

The entertaining and engaging aspect of the role of bartender was the first trait I noticed in those behind the bar. It was fascinating to see how easily they seemed to rile-up the natives to create an exciting atmosphere.

There was another side to some of the bartenders that I witnessed at the bar, however; an element of compassion, perhaps. They resembled some of the animal trainers I've worked with at times, in that they knew there was some controversy surrounding their job, but also that there was no one else out there better fit to care and sympathize for the creatures under their watch.

The bartenders in this study seemed to walk a thin boundary between vice and virtue. Realistically, they encouraged their visitors to soak their livers with poison. But on the other side of that reality exists a unique bond and an element of sincere understanding between the two parties. For instance, I saw a bartender refuse to serve one of the natives, simply because he felt as if it would be a threat to their safety. There have been many times in the wild where I wanted to intervene in order to save a cute, tiny creature from certain death—yet my job was to film it being eaten. Granted, that is an extreme scenario, but at times, the bartenders appeared to be conflicted in terms of ethics of their role, and the well-being of the frequenters at the watering hole.

***

When I first began to consider tending bar as a way to make money, I imagined myself having a blast in the company of friends and making a decent amount of cash while doing so. I visualized many a night that would end with women slipping me their phone numbers on cocktail napkins or being up on the bar pouring tequila down an array of bursting bras. And although some of those dreams eventually came true, the job hasn't proven to be all fun and games.

Alcohol, in excess, is pretty bad for you. It kills the body and can, at times, do the same to your finances. The drinkable ethanol that we love so much often finds its way to the scene of domestic disputes as well as horrific car accidents. And who knows how many accidental pregnancies were the direct result of having one too many?

In essence, our job as a bartender is to serve people something that has a significant chance of ruining their lives or even killing them. We reason with this by saying that if we don't do it, someone else will. We justify what we do by singling out the cutthroat economy we live in and our need to pay for school, or kids, or school *for* kids.

But as bartenders, we do a lot more than pour beers and mix cocktails. We are therapists, storytellers, networking connections for the newbies in town, absorbers of many a pick-up line, comedians, and sports analysts. But above all, we are friends—temporary or long-lasting—that arrive to work to enhance your day, night, week, month, or year. With a little help from a buzz, we are there to try our best to send you out the door feeling better about yourself than you did when you walked in. Even the most seasoned and cranky bartender will get that warm and gooey feeling after knowing they made someone happy during a shift.

Furthermore, most of us know that going out and blowing-off steam is a great thing to do every now and then. Blowing off that steam incorporates some shots and beers, good friends, dancing, drunkenly singing songs out loud that we only know half of the lyrics to, eating greasy pub food, and even taking home a *four* or a *five* for a one-night stand can be just what the doctor ordered to relieve stress. However, when you see the same faces from behind the bar five, six, or even seven days a week, an internal conflict can arise.

Should Bartenders Give A Damn?

As much as we are tempted to chime in as life coaches to our beloved bar guests, it is not necessarily our place or role to do so. When an uber-obese guy pulls two bar stools together—one for each ass cheek—and orders a double-vodka with Red Rull paired with a loaded burger with extra bacon and cheese on his fries, I'm inclined to smack him across his jiggly face and ask him if he's actually *trying* to kill himself.

But as a bartender—an employee of a business—I am there to tell him how delicious and succulent the burger is and to reward his decision to double-up on his bacon intake with a high-five and a compliment—ya know, something generic and gross along the lines of "Excellent choice, sir!" It's hurtful and I often feel ashamed after the fact.

This beached whale will sit there and spill his heart out about how he got shit-canned from the military for being unfit for duty and how his wife just left him, all the while licking his fingers clean of bacon grease and chugging down cheap vodka and sugary energy drinks. What is a drink slinger to do in this case? Do you say *no, fatty! I'm not going to be your grim reaper! I'm not going to be the one who serves you your inevitable killer heart attack or incurable diabetes on a plate*? Of course not, for that would surely be the fastest and most direct route to the unemployment line.

Although you may not think it's a good idea to serve this pathetic and self-loathing guy such unhealthy garbage that would clog his arteries even more, it isn't really a bartender's role to convince him that he should choose a salad and glass of wine instead.

Bartender VS Shrink

Bartenders can act as a type of band aid to those with personal problems and no medical insurance to fund a conventional consultation for those problems. Now, we're not as classically or formally trained as certified therapists, but what we lack in formality we make up for in improvisation and a perverted view of looking at the world. Allow me to explain.

Think about it. Going to a therapist can be an ego-crushing experience at first, especially if you've been a model citizen your whole life. Although I think it would healthy for everyone to see a therapist on a regular basis, in our society, taking a day off of work to see the shrink makes others look at you with an awkward eye.

185

Once arrived, you walk into the well-organized, spotless office and take a seat on an expensive leather chair. As you look around the room at all of the degrees, certificates, and awards fastened on the walls, you begin to feel even more small and ashamed. You're about to discuss your problems with a squared-away winner—a well-educated go-getter

It just so happens that some people feel more comfortable vomiting their issues to the bartender who's covered in tattoos and has been arrested a handful of times; a person who's traveled the world, has volumes of sexcapades under his belt, and has logged exponentially more hours listening to guests' problems than the almost $200 per hour psychiatrist with a Ph.D.

I think that this preference is reasonably justifiable. It's obvious that you won't be getting (at least not purposely getting) top-notch feedback in accordance with well-documented and published psychological theory, but rather a comfortable and casual space, a cold beer, and a bartender's ear to talk into—a bartender who's most likely seen, heard, and done way more more fucked-up shit than you could ever imagine.

But, when amateur psychological warfare doesn't do the trick and you start seeing this poor soul's long and sad face more and more, a red flag shoots up and flaps in the whirlwind of mental skirmish and judgment as you hand them a temporary solution to what you know is a long-term problem.

Move Over Dr. Phil

I once served a gentleman who couldn't really decide on what to drink. He had strolled in around happy hour during the middle of the week, and the confused, lost look on his face paired with his slow and unsure selection of a barstool caught my attention.

He seemed overwhelmed and uncomfortable. When I greeted him it was still slow before getting busy shortly after. I asked him if he wanted to see the beer list, and when he asked me what we had on draft, I gently pointed to the list that I had already placed in front of him.

"Can I have a glass of Miller Lite," he politely asked with a touch of insecurity to his voice.

I thought to myself "Who the hell asks for a *glass* of beer?" A glass of wine, yeah. But a beer comes in bottles, pints, goblets, and even boots—not glasses.

I poured him a brewski and quickly forgot about him. Time was flying that night and I was mainly working the other side of the bar. A little while later I opened his tab from the other terminal and saw that he was three Miller Lites deep. Before long, he was at five. Now, he wasn't necessarily a small guy, nor was he that big. But I saw him struggle to get off of his barstool and then perform a zombie walk as he made his way towards the door. Aside from a toddler, perhaps, five Miller's shouldn't get you drunk.

I spotted it at the same time as my manager, Teenie. I ran out from behind the bar and we created a blockade of sorts —we wanted him to have to go through us in order to use the front exit. We politely asked him if he'd like a cab. He said that he was fine. We verbally disagreed.

"Sir, you really shouldn't be driving."

He looked like he was about to puke and pass out at the same time, so we got him to sit down and drink some water. Teenie was furious with me for over-serving him, as there were loads of families coming into the pub for dinner time. But when I told her how much he had, she put the claws away.

"Five Miller Lites...what the fuck?" she questioned to herself under her breath as she walked away.

Now, I've had people react the same way after two cocktails. Usually, it becomes known that it was due to some strange reaction to medication that the guest is on that doesn't mix well with alcohol. But in this case, we found out that this guy was new—or at least making a comeback—to the drinking game.

I sat outside with him for just a minute as the happy hour crowd started to leave, which gave us some breathing room before the late-night rush. He was mumbling something about being a bad father and a bad husband—basically an all-around shitbag. I put him in the cab and wished him well. I thought nothing more of it.

He came back the next day...and the day after that...and the day after that. He came in two weeks straight, four-to-five days per week, and seemed absolutely determined to get sloppy each time. During a slow period, I finally got a chance to talk to the guy before he had enough to zap him of his motor skills. I made small talk with him, searching for the right time to drop the bomb and tell him we were going to have to 86 him if he continued to get so drunk. He divulged —quite openly—that he'd never been a drinker, but since being laid off from work, he had been feeling off. He then told me that his wife was incredible and so were his kids.

Usually it's the other way around, in that the guest is trying to *escape* his or her wretched family in search of a few pints, some sports talk, or just some time to just sit there and think. But this guy was different. He couldn't stop raving about how amazing his family was. His son was captain of this and president of that. His daughter has been the lead in the school play three years in a row. His wife was a successful nurse and marathon runner. They even bred dogs. All of it sounded great to me, but not all was well upstairs in his head.

I began to detect a bit of a masochistic tone to him. I suspected that he was embarrassed of himself. He felt like less of a man because he was now out of work. He had no hobbies, so he ended up just sitting around the house, bored and lonely, looking for some type of stimulation. He had nothing going on and felt like a deadbeat compared to his overachieving family, so he turned to the local watering hole in an attempt to feel better about himself—to find that lacking stimulation. He actually admitted that he was home watching reruns of the show *Cheers* and thought it would be a good idea to find a group like that to belong to.

I noticed the bags under his eyes taking up more of his face with each passing day. I also noticed that he went from dressing in clean, well-pressed office attire to a sleeveless shirt, gym shorts, flip-flops, and a 30-year-old-looking baseball hat that, when he wore it low, casted a shadow over his now scruffy face. He looked like he was swirling down the shitter.

I finally had a breakthrough with him one day, though. This day was different from the rest because I had just gotten back from surfing and decided to stop at the pub on my way home for a cold one. You'll never guess who was there! The bar was empty at the time, so I sat next to our man of mystery just to be courteous and welcoming being that I did indeed work there. But as we clinked glasses, I felt like prying a bit.

"So what's up with you, man," I inquired curiously but with a touch of humor to my tone.

"What?"

"I said, what's up with you?"

"What do you mean," he asked innocently.

"C'mon dude, you know what I mean. The first day you came in here you resembled Bambi looking for his mother or something. Now you're a barroom pro. What's up?"

I think he was nervous, caught off guard, and maybe even a bit insulted by my question, but after gathering his thoughts for a few seconds, he gave me an answer.

"I want to be a good father. I want to be a good husband. But I'm out of work. I'm unemployed and I can't buy my kids jack-shit right now…and my wife—" he paused, looked the other direction to collect himself, and then took a sip of his *glass* of beer before continuing. "I'm afraid of losing her. She's amazing and I feel inadequate now. I'm afraid of letting her down...letting everyone down...even the dogs. Something like that."

The hard-nosed side of me wanted to punch him in the arm and tell him to man the fuck up! I wanted to tally up all of the overpriced beer that he'd had during the past month at the bar and scold him for not using that money to buy his boy new soccer spikes, or his little girl tickets to a play on Broadway, or his wife a night out on the town. I wanted to drop him down for push-ups for feeling so sorry for himself. *Pathetic. What a whiny little bitch.*

My eyes ended up straying towards Kat and the cocktail she was making behind the bar. I glanced at the word "compassion" that's tattooed across her wrist. I had seen it many times before, but in that moment of searching for the right way to react to this guy's dilemma, I saw it in a more profound light.

I ended up taking a page from Kat's book and compassion'd the shit out of this guy. I said what I had to. I listened, I analyzed, and then I chimed in. I suggested to him that his kids could probably care less whether or not he's working right now. If anything, they're probably happy to have him around the house more. Dad is always the hero, and when kids see their father—their own personal hero—start to slip and become nervous and vulnerable, they become nervous and vulnerable as well.

As far as his wife was concerned, I understood the fact that he felt like less of a man because she was now the one earning the bread right. But I told him to think about what it was like when she bore the two kids. I was willing to bet that

191

he was pulling overtime shifts so that she could rest in bed and recover without worry.

A marriage is a partnership you nitwit. There's nothing attractive or sexy about self-pity. Now fix yourself and be sexy for your wife, I said with my mind.

Then I spoke with actual words.

"Look man, you gotta get your shit together, and that's not going to happen here. You've had your time away from your family to reflect here on this barstool with your *glasses* of Miller Lite, but it's time to fix this. I think you've been your own worst enemy and really have given yourself an unneeded beating. It's good to get out of the house every now and again and do your own thing. There's also nothing wrong with having a beer and shooting the shit with your bartender. But remember—we're just bartenders. Although we may have moments of brilliance, most of us are trying to figure out our own shit."

"Yeah, I hear ya," he said with a big sigh. "I don't even like Miller Lite."

We both chuckled at his comment before I continued.

"Dude, your family just misses you. I don't even know them, but I'm sure they miss you being around. If you keep screwing off here, they might begin to take offense. Especially the dogs."

After my buzzed pep talk, he seemed refreshed and re-born, almost as if he was going to get up and sing a pre-choreographed opera piece like Adam Sandler in *Billy Madison* about what he needed to do to get his life back on track.

He quickly requested his tab like a pro—ya know the cursive "z" in the air—rather than yelling for the *barkeep's* attention. I told him that he needed to go home, reclaim his role as the hero, pick his kids up and swing them around in the air until they get nauseous, and remind them that you love them and are there for them always. I told him that he needed to go home and have an intimate night with his wife, and remind her that he's a partner in their marriage, and that during his furlough he'll be taking care of everything around the house and supporting her in any way that he can. I told him to remind her that he's a part of the same team with the same purpose, not just two individuals living together who occasionally have sex and share a bank account. Oh, and I told him to stop at the store on the way home and buy his dogs the biggest, most delicious bones that he could find.

Then, after he got up and left (very abruptly, mind you, and without really even thanking me or anything, which I found quite odd), one of our other regulars sent me a shot and jokingly asked if he could schedule an appointment with "Dr. Jay." I laughed as I raised my glass and thanked him, and laughed some more as I imagined what Deloris would have said if she had been there...*Yeah, Dr. Jay, can I schedule a full body exam with you soon? How about an enema...with your PENIS?!*

Eat that, Dr. Phil.

12

Rage

There are rules to this ecosystem just like anywhere else. And if you break enough of these rules, you'll likely be exiled from the pack like a male lion who just lost a battle to a younger challenger. Some of these rules are no-brainers, while others are more subtle and learned. I was barked and yelled at several times for my own infractions, which made me feel like I did as a kid when I innocently-enough fed my dog a chocolate bar in its entirety. I didn't know what I had done wrong.

During my experience observing the watering hole, I was able to somewhat decipher the laws of this strange land. There are many, and for that, I decided to approach the bartenders and document some of the things that anger them the most. They tend to be quick to anger, and so the list is long.

***

The curse of tending bar balances its blessing. On some days, it's a job that doesn't seem like a job at all, but rather a fun night out that you get paid for. On other days, it's a job that can leave you feeling stressed and over your head like Arnold

Schwarzenegger in *Kindergarten Cop* after dealing with ankle-biting kids all day.

In the context of gripes, tending bar is very similar to any other job in which one deals with the public on a daily basis. I'm sure that police officers, customer service representatives at the nearest Walmart, bell-hops, teachers, nurses, and bankers all crowd around each other at the end of their shift to bitch and moan about all of the assholes, tightwads, and all-around impossible people that they had to put-up with on that particular day. They form a circle in the break room or at the bar after work and rant until they are hoarse, flinging their cigarette butts at the ground and their flailing arms in the air in disgust. They foam at the mouth as they try to describe how some twatty customer, patient, or student turned their day into a living hell.

A tale is told of a commuter who dished out a disturbing amount of attitude and insults to a highway patrol officer (who two hours earlier was helping clean up an accident scene where an entire young family was killed) for pulling him over for his malfunctioning taillight.

A nurse, at the end of back-to-back-to-back eighteen hour shifts and on the verge of tears, questions aloud with desperation to her fellow overworked comrades just how people could be so mean and insensitive to others who are trying to care for them.

Department store retail workers protest the constant bombardment of abuse that they receive from disgruntled customers, as if an employee who gets paid $8.50 per hour has *anything* to do with company return policy or null and void coupons that were misinterpreted by the consumer.

Teachers pull their hair out as they exchange horror stories of having to deal with obsessive and unrealistic parents as well as their snot-nosed, bratty little kids.

It's an all-out frenzy, and just like the poor and aggravated souls mentioned above, bartenders love few things more than having a beer after work and ravenously jabbering about all of the impatient, cheap, and difficult guests that they encountered that night. Bartenders are the undisputed champs of over-the-top tirades about pain-in-the-ass customers.

The following examples and scenarios are what really bring about our ire and tempts us to pick up the ice pick. They have been compiled by bartenders and servers whom I've had the pleasure of working with over the years, and are meant to provoke some thought—perhaps even hesitation— the next time you find yourself snapping your fingers at the guy or gal behind the bar. Ack-rite, and you'll be taken good care of.

Tonsil Hockey

Your drunken tongue wrestling match ten inches from the bartender is repulsive (unless you're two hot girls, of course). We don't need nor want to see you tilting your head back and forth as you try to swallow your partner's head— *especially* if it's closing time and you haven't paid your tab yet. Our spill mats are there to catch excess booze and juice, not the streams of saliva that you're flicking around the room with your tongue.

I think the best story I've heard of lovebirds swapping spit at the bar was that of a resourceful server who stole a dildo from a bachelorette party's table and slapped it down on the bar directly in front of the couple, resulting in an eruption of laughter and bright-red faces.

It's interesting to note that the rubber sex toy went missing shortly after. Neither the bachelorette party or any of the bar's employees admitted to confiscating it. Having said that, everyone had a pretty good idea where it probably ended up.

Know What You Want!

There are few things more that a bar guest does that can disrupt the flow of a bartender more than not being clear about what it is that they want. This can range from calling the 'barmaid's' attention and not having their drink order ready upon acknowledgment, to making her do wind sprints back and forth behind the bar because they want to add an additional drink to their order.

It's four deep at the bar and the drink slingers are cranking. Guests are trying to shove their way to the front of the wall of bodies like Black Friday shoppers pushing their way into Best Buy to snatch the door buster deal. It's a chaotic experience for the bartender who's trying to navigate the sea of whistling guests and protruding arms frantically waiving money, credit cards, and empty glasses.

When the bartender acts as the mother pelican with a fresh catch protruding from its beak ready to feed its young, it can be a difficult decision as to which hungry, crying baby bird to feed first. She scans the crowd trying to select the next guest to accommodate. Taking into account appearance, posture, eye-contact, availability of money or credit card, and the estimated order of arrival, the decision is made.

A man in his late 20s is up next. He has his money out and is not waving it flagrantly like those surrounding him. He's making eye contact with the bartender but not yelling or whistling for attention. He seems like the proper selection for the next guest to be served.

"What can I get for you?"

"Uh, give me a Jack and diet, and—"

He hesitates and follows with one of the most hated phrases ever heard by a busy, pressed, and stressed bartender. "Hold on."

HOLD ON? OK! Cut! Stop production! I have to hold on! A collective groan now spreads throughout the bar crowd, a shared annoyance from the rest who wait to have their glasses filled.

"Yo, what do you guys want," he asks as he turns his head toward his spaced-out friends, now becoming aware of the disdain growing for him from both sides of the bar.

"Gimme two Coors lights too." As the bartender charges towards the Coors light tap and maneuvers around her co-workers like Barry Sanders avoiding tackles, she returns with two pints of beer for the guest who already has one strike against him. She then informs him of the balance due.

"My bad, lemme get one more." He's now drawn a huge amount of negative attention to himself, and most likely will be put on the shit list for the rest of the evening.

During these precious moments of ambivalence, the bartender has missed out on putting a few more greenbacks into the cash drawer and tip jar all because she had to wait for this guy to make up his mind.

For this, you can bet that the next time he approaches the bar in search of a drink or two, he's going to wait until everyone who has followed proper bar etiquette has been served first. It might not necessarily be a matter of spite, but more so a question of economics. You cater to those who keep the cash flow going. You do business with those who don't cause you more of a headache than is called for. A plumber will always choose a job with a little less monetary reward but that brings about less stress, rather than a job that will put a little more coin in his pocket but will also have him deal with a customer looking over his shoulder all day, asking "What does that do? What is that for?"

On a quiet night at the grocery store, it's fine and dandy to have a conversation with the produce guy about the local farm that has recently become the vendor for red and green peppers, or to ask questions about which fillet of fish would go better with the marinade you just put into your basket. But, c'mon—this is America! Use a little common sense and have some awareness of the urgency that the rest of the customers have. If there's a long line, use your waiting time to decide on what you want, and if you do have curious thoughts about the fish, try and come up with a concise question that can be answered quickly, as to not hold up the rest of the line.

The same principle applies at the bar. Scan the area for a beer menu if you don't know what's on draft. Do your research, and if you have a question, it better be a quick one. When it's four people deep at the circle bar with thirsty guests and crisp twenty dollar bills being held up in their hands, your bartender doesn't have the excess time to have an in-depth discussion with you about what kind of malt was used to make the local IPA.

To make your and everyone else's experience out at the bar a little more enjoyable, have a good idea of what you want when it is your turn to order. Also, have a backup plan. If you want a Tanqueray and tonic, think about what you might be interested in if the Tanqueray supply were to run dry. As in life, it's always a good idea to have a contingency plan.

What Do You Guys Have On Draft?

I love this one: Some drunk and aloof guys come stumbling in the door, walk up to the bar (where I greet them *through* the tap handles), and ask me "Hey, what do you guys have on draft?"

"...Uh, these ones...," I articulate slowly as I wave my hand over them like a magician who just pulled a rabbit from his hat.

Coins

Coins. We don't want them! When you leave me chump change on the bar and wink at me and say "that's for you chief," you can rest assured that I am trying to murder you with my mind. I cannot yell loud enough from the highest mountaintop how much bartenders absolutely loath receiving coins as tips. It's a monumental slap in the face, an insult of the highest degree.

I'm busy. I'm very busy. Tonight is $1.00 Miller lite night, and the guests at the watering hole are converging on me from all sides. Driven mad by their thirst for the triple hops-brewed pilsner that is so very affordable on this particular evening, they shout and lunge at me from all sides. I'm surrounded, under duress, and dripping with sweat from the many wind-sprints I've been making to the Miller tap for the past several hours.

"Yo, uhh, lemme get four Millah lites and a vodka n' cranberry," says a guy with thicker neck and biceps than his Long Island accent. I sprint back and forth, dodging the waving arms of restless guests trying to jab and poke at me for my attention, and place four M*illah lites* and a vodka and cranberry in front of this Affliction t-shirt-sporting Neanderthal. "That will be $9.50, please." And yes, I always say please.

"Here ya go boss, the rest is for you," he said proudly as he dropped my tip onto the bar top.

As I saw two pathetic and far-from-shiny quarters laying on the bar where this dipshit once stood, a rage welled-up inside of me.

That's it.

I stopped serving drinks and immediately embodied the character of an elderly peasant—the village drunkard—perhaps during a fit of dementia, as I stood crooked and doubled-over, waving and calling out for this guy's attention.

"Thank you, Gov'nah," I yelped in a voice similar to Will Ferrell's character from the Saturday Night Live skit, *The Old Prospector*. I pretended to chase him down what would-be the cobblestone roads of the town square, thanking him for his charitable donation to my coin dish.

"Thank you Gov'nah so very much indeed! With your generous contribution, I clamber closer to having the means necessary to construct a sign that reads 'The drinks are cheap so you don't have to be!'" My sarcastic rant ended there, but not before I threw the coins at him. Surprisingly, I missed his gigantic lats and nailed the back wall instead. *Oops. I missed. I never miss.*

He turned and looked at me with a startled and confused expression on his face, and then turned once more to continue on with his night, as did the groaning, thirsty undead.

Was I a bit out of line? Probably. But fuck it—he had it coming, and I needed to blow off my pent-up rage before I was to jab someone's eyeballs out with an olive skew. When a bartender is pouring drinks on full throttle and is depending on tips as a means of compensation, you immediately place yourself at the bottom rung of the food chain when you shower us with your not-so-precious metals.

Smartphone Mixologist

The ability to quickly search a drink recipe that has escaped your memory, via smartphone, is a revolutionary tactic for bartenders. What makes us want to take *your* smartphone and dump into your *Pan Galactic Gargle Blaster*, however, is when you search the depths of the internet for obscure drink recipes such as...a Pan Galactic Gargle Blaster, and expect us to be your entertainment monkey by making such a stupid drink. Credit to Danny on this one.

Why Aren't You Smiling?!

Has anyone ever asked you this question during a bad day at work? Didn't it just make you want to shatter their orbital bones with your fists? Yeah...how 'bout that...

To those of you who ask this question to coworkers or, in this case, to your bartenders or servers—go to hell you condescending bag of douche! *You're* the reason I'm not smiling. Your drink, your smell, your clothes, your questions, your face—all of it casts a shadow over my sunny day. Everything about you takes the jam out of my doughnut. Eat shit. Credit to Chelsea 'O' for her rage on this one.

Napkin and Coaster Shredding

Holy hell, people. This annoying and mess-making habit definitely ranks high on the list of things that pisses your bartender off the most.

There is an almost infinite amount of behavioral ticks that the human nervous system convinces the body into performing. Imagine the brain as the puppeteer, and the body's fingers, arms, legs, face, and eyes as the puppets. When you fold your arms, excessively lick your lips, or tap your foot, your body is executing all of the commands brought to those particular areas of your body by motor cells.

We all do it. No one is innocent when it comes to committing this act of obsessive-compulsive destruction. Occasionally, it can actually be quite cute. It goes beyond the border of cuteness and into the land of annoyance, however, when it results in an absolute mess.

Go into the supermarket, walk up behind the kid whose bagging groceries and start ripping all of his brown paper bags to shreds. Then, pile all of the pieces on the rubber conveyor belt at the register. Good luck with not getting punched in the face by this high school junior who realizes he's seventeen years of age and can legally get away with punching you in the eye.

Bartenders usually don't care if you take coasters nor do they care what the label on your beer bottle looks like once you've finished it. It's just a pain in the ass to clean up, a completely unnecessary chore to perform. Not to mention the bar top tends to become wet and sticky throughout the course of a busy night, no matter how much one wipes it down. Add to those wet spots hundreds of small paper fragments and you have one hell of a clean-up job at the end of the night.

Move!

We bipedal talking monkeys seem to be losing our sense of awareness at an exponential pace. It has become a common sight to observe someone texting on their smartphone while walking across the street, somehow comfortable enough with the idea that the person behind the wheel of a two-ton hunk of metal (also texting) headed in their direction is going to stop for them at the crosswalk.

The clueless pedestrian continues to type away with their thumbs as their trust of a commuting normality guides them into the road without even looking up. This amazes me. Does sending a text at that exact moment supersede one's instinct to avoid danger and remain alive? In this new generation of distracting mobile devices, it seems that people have increasingly begun to ignore their basic sense of their surroundings—an elementary instinct that propelled us through past evolutionary stages until now.

It could be a case of overcrowding as well, but I find myself always getting bumped into or barely avoiding collision with men and women pushing shopping carts at the supermarket. My grocery shopping usually consists of purchasing ten to fifteen items, all placed neatly in a small basket which I carry at my side throughout the building. The majority of shoppers, however, push large shopping carts, sometimes filled to the brim and then some, all while looking everywhere and in every direction except the one they're traveling in. To the left, to the right, up, down; they scour the shelves for their favorite cereal, cooking spices, and toilet paper—completely oblivious to those other shoppers around them. I stutter-step, slide, and spin my way out of danger while trying to keep my carton of eggs unbroken.

You can always spot the shoppers who work in a restaurant, however. They move through crowds of erratic gawkers with ease and finesse, as they are used to cautiously snaking their way around unaware dining guests while protecting a tray of $40.00 shots of Johnny Walker Blue, or scolding hot bowls of soup.

Bartenders, servers, shot girls, food runners, and bussers all have a heightened sense of awareness of their relative positioning amongst the crowd, even under the influence of the many drugs that restaurant employees are known to be on during a shift. I often touch people on their shoulders and lower backs while saying "behind" to them, to notify them of my close proximity. I do this at home, at the bank, at the store—just about everywhere.

My point is to rant about the most frustrating and performance-hindering crimes committed by guests at the drinking establishment, or any kind of restaurant for that matter—*not moving out of the way!*

In a busy bar, it is imperative that the employees move quickly and efficiently as to not fall behind on service. This includes the delivery of food from the cook's line in the kitchen to the cocktail tables outside on the patio. It includes the servers' ability to pick up and drop off drinks in a timely manner. And it includes the bartender's or barback's capacity to escape from the bar and change an empty keg, or carry and deliver a fresh case of beer to their coworkers.

A 130 pound hustling barback, drenched in sweat and his stomach growling from lack of nutrition, carries more than half his body weight as he balances three 30-packs through the moving sea of guests dancing to the DJ's beats. He yells politely, directing people to "make a hole, please!" But alas; it's to no avail. He's bumped into, stepped on, and drinks are spilled on him as people begin to acknowledge his existence, almost viewing him as a villain.

With no other option available, and after noticing from across the room the bartender's anxiety, frustration, and sense of urgency, he pushes his scrawny bones through an awkward make-out session—tongues flying everywhere. He then takes a flying elbow to the face from a big guy who's engaged in a drunken dance-off with a friend.

But he's almost there! Hang on little buddy! He's almost arrived to his pinned-down brothers-in-arms, carrying with him precious supplies that are desperately needed at this point of the night. With a few pinches on his ass from an older couple that has been seen swinging there before, our valiant squire finally arrives at the bar with the goods, just in the nick of time. Of course, he ritualistically and expectedly gets chewed-out by his bartender for taking so long, but gets a pat on the back and a brief *thank you* right before being sent out over the wire again.

This kid's already difficult task would have been less difficult if these fleshy obstacles had made just an ounce of effort to get out of the way for him. I understand that these culinary ninjas usually dressed in black can sneak-up on even the most Jedi of people, but when you realize that he's there and needs to get by you, do the humane thing and get out of his way. If you see that he's trying to get by someone else with four large buckets of ice and no free hands to tap someone's shoulders, take a second away from your conversation and notify that person that they're in the way. A small gesture like that is always greatly appreciated. Hell, you may even get a free drink out of it.

Move, people. If you see a delivery man pushing a cart full of packages into an office complex, move out of his way—or better yet, hold the door for him! If you're driving the speed limit or below in the left lane on the highway, don't be a self-absorbed boob and stay there angrily mumbling to yourself about how you don't like it when people tailgate you. *Move over!* And please, please, pleaseeeee—if you see a restaurant employee trying to finagle their way around a crowd, help them out a bit by moving out of their way and suggesting to others to do the same. It will be appreciated more than you know.

Service Bar

No amount of signs, turnbuckle belts, verbal instructions, or bouncers seem able to keep the herd of thirsty bar guests away from service bar. This line of defense always breaks on a busy Friday or Saturday night, and it's an extremely annoying obstacle that a server, bartender, or barback faces during a shift.

Service bar is a designated area for the employees to conduct internal business. All of those drinks you see at tables and cocktail high-tops come from service bar. If you clog the traffic lanes and disrupt the organization of the service bar area, you're essentially screwing with the other folks' experience at the watering hole. You're a cancerous tumor to the innocent cells throughout the body of the room.

Asking a busy bartender who is cranking on service bar for a drink is like asking a fireman who's hosing down a five-alarm fire to help you get your kitten out of the tree. That goes for friends, family, cops, politicians, and celebrities. Move along, please. Not only is the bartender who's stationed at service bar concerned with keeping up with service tickets, but they have to manage the order, position, and eventual extraction of each drink.

You're not that important. In fact, your level of importance drops the more you pester the employees encircled around the already chaotic service bar. Climbing under the security tape and moving the meticulously placed drinks off of their designated tickets to make room for your elbow as you casually lean in to check out the cleavage of one of the cocktail servers—yeah; not cool. Find another spot to be creepy. You're fucking up the environment with your grime.

Separate Checks

Times are tough. Our economy is struggling as the average Joe is trying to secure some type of stability in the workplace and in their bank account. Also, less and less people are paying daily transactions with cash nowadays, which can pose a problem when out to dinner with company at the time to pay the bill—especially if the party exceeds six people.

When bar customers pay with credit instead of everyone throwing cash into one big pile on the table, it ends up being a huge pain the in ass for the server to separate each item onto individual checks. It often hinders their ability to efficiently serve their other guests.

I remember seeing a party of thirty-or-so military personnel request separate checks at the *end* of the night. Now, it's widely agreed upon that our uniformed men and women aren't paid nearly enough for what they do for a living, but that shouldn't be taken out on the 19-year-old waitress who's working all summer long to afford college tuition.

If you don't feel like tapping the ATM, and your party insists on separate checks, it's a good idea to inform your server or bartender *beforehand*. Nowadays, most bars have fairly advanced point of sale systems that allow for the separation of checks throughout the evening. This idea of preemptive notification goes for coupons as well. This way, the server can plan to adjust the check during a slow break in the action.

If you bomb the poor guy or gal with a request for thirty separate checks—all including at least a beer or two, an appetizer, and an entrée—you're setting them up for failure and being a complete turd. It can take a while to process that request, and as they do so, the other guests that are sitting at their designated tables of service end up looking around with an expression of abandonment and disapproval. Their tip will eventually suffer as a consequence of your party's ignorance.

It's a matter of common sense, folks. The universe doesn't revolve around you and your party. There are others in the house who expect prompt and efficient service, and with the ol' last-minute separate check request, you're really holding up the show.

Coupons

If you hold-up the line because you want to ensure that you get a dollar off here and a few cents off there, you're an asshole. I remember when I worked as a cashier at the supermarket when I was younger and used to bring my own change to work just to please all of the old hags and cheap mongrels that demanded an extra penny or nickel back from their transaction.

Servers and bartenders are often hurt by coupons. What many visitors to the watering hole don't understand is the idea of proportionate tipping.

If I have a buy one/get one free coupon for a loaf of bread, no one is really harmed by the utilization of that coupon. Basically, the fat cats at corporate headquarters taking a break from the workday to practice back flips into their

Olympic-sized pools of money, decided to offer coupons for that specific loaf of bread because they're most likely having trouble selling all of it. They end up throwing out what's left over anyway.

But using a coupon to eliminate 30% off of a restaurant bill shouldn't mean you shave 30% off of gratuity. Is it fair to tip a fraction of what you normally would have if there was no coupon? The server or bartender, in most cases, doesn't make any income from the itemized list of goods consumed. Again, we work for tips.

If you use a coupon for 30% off on a $100 check, you end up being charged for $70. Instead of leaving a $15-20 tip, you squeal like a piggy in excitement as you realize you don't have to leave that much! You let out a deafening burp as you wrestle the wallet out of your stretched-out jeans. You place a $7 tip on the table instead. You're happy because you feel like you won.

Maybe you did win, but you did so by cheating, you fuckface. The server should not make less money because you ended up saving money from a coupon. They did the same amount of work as they would have done if the bill ended up being $100. If you can't afford to tip appropriately as per today's social norm of 15-20%, then stay the fuck home. You're screwing someone else over by taking advantage of a "deal." In that case, I hope you choke on your two-for-one rack of ribs, fatty.

Hey Barkeep!

Hey boss! Champ! Buddy! Chief! Guy! Skippy! Bartender! Barmaid! Barkeep! Yo! Yo! Hey! Yo!

SHUT THE FUCK UPPPPPPPPPP!

Whatever happened to *excuse me, pardon me, sir, mam,* and other polite ways of interacting with strangers in public and gaining their attention?

You see it happen in movies and on television all the time: the protagonist, dressed nicely in a well-tailored suit, leans casually and confidently up against the bar top, halfway turned to the bar and halfway looking out towards the room, scanning for his rendezvous target.

"Bartender," he yells sternly, as if he's calling for his dog to bring him the newspaper. "Two fingahs of ya finest scotch."

"Right away, sir," the bartender obediently responds, all but getting on his knees and bowing to the imposing and audacious figure. The bartender obliges by neatly placing his scotch in front of him. *Sellout.*

That's bullshit. The only way you'll get away with talking to me like that is if you're swishing $100s into my tip jar. And even then, I'll let you know about it once those Benjamins are in my pocket.

Your bartender is not your errand boy, so it would behoove you to not address him as such. Don't snap your fingers or wave your hand around in the air like you do at hockey games to get the t-shirt cannon guy to fire in your direction. Don't shout out any of the ridiculous pet names listed above. Doing so is to place yourself on the shit list.

Want to know how to get a drink at a crowded bar? Have your money or credit card handy, make eye contact, and be ready to place your drink order. Tip well the first go-round, and if your bartender has any sense at all, you're glass will be swooped-up quickly for another drink the next time it's empty.

Personally, I just don't put up with the pet names anymore. I will immediately let it be known that I will not respond to such name-calling. "Yes, customer" is how I typically answer back. That, or I simply play the ignore game until they realize what a dick they're being and ask for my attention in a civilized manner.

What's your cheapest beer?

Just get out—it's over.

That question just painted a big scarlet letter on your forehead as a cheapskate. It's already been written in scripture that there is no hope for you in being a decent tipper. And if there's some *Slingblade*-ish deep twang to your voice, it will probably make your bartender see you as a threat to the peace and comfort of all of the docile creatures at the watering hole—they'll see you as the hyena that wandered into an area being enjoyed by mellow antelope and grazing giraffe.

A real estate agent isn't going to waste time dealing with someone who looks and acts like they're ready to move out of their cardboard box and into a storage container. If your wallet is home to many a moth and few greenbacks, first try scanning the room for posters that display the drink specials. If none are visible, you're best bet is to just order a light domestic beer on draft. Draft tends to be cheaper than bottle. Domestic is usually cheaper than import. Just don't ask us what our cheapest beer is, OK? You're not flattering yourself when you inquire such a thing.

Do You Want To Start A Tab?

By now, it shouldn't be a secret to anyone that cash is king. Cash is what makes the world go 'round. From children buying and selling candy to each other on the playground, to international drug or weapons dealers, to yard sales—cash is still, as of now, the recommended method of payment at the watering hole.

When buying your first round of drinks at the bar, you're usually prompted with the option to either pay cash at each point of sale or to start a tab. In this day and age, a credit card is usually required to start a tab with the bar. The order is entered into the computer, the card is swiped by the bartender, and then it is either stowed away behind the bar or given back to the guest. What this does is it files the credit card information in the system and basically acts as a deposit or insurance policy against someone walking out without paying. If that happens, the card is charged no matter what and the bartender/house doesn't lose out. There's nothing worse than working all night and having to pay for someone's tab that got sloppy and forgot to pay before leaving.

If you are using a credit card, *please start a tab if you plan on having more than one drink!* Even if you're not planning on it (unless there's a large minimum, which is common at nightclubs and tourist destinations). If you're not one-hundred percent positive that you'll be leaving after that one drink, start a tab with your bartender.

For every swipe of the magnetic strip on the back of your card—for every transaction—the house has to pay a fee. The annoyance isn't limited to just that, because for every transaction made with plastic, there's a transaction slip to catalog into the system, more paper that needs to be printed, organized and stapled, etc.

It doesn't cost you anything extra to start a tab at the bar, and it's very, very uncommon (I won't say it's impossible because mistakes do happen) that they'll lose your card or give it away to someone else.

You Touch—You Buy!

This gripe correlates directly with the prior piece about starting tabs, and is probably the one occurrence that burns my ass the most.

What citizen of these United States of 'Murica would be any less than enraged by someone who avoids paying for a provided service? Communists, I say!

When I stir and pour a Manhattan or shake and strain a French 75 into your glass, I am providing to you a product and a service for which I am expecting to be compensated for.

All too often, guests have the inclination to walk away without paying for my carefully crafted cocktail and head towards their table in the dining room. For some odd reason, there exists this misconception that it's OK to do this. Well I'll tell you that it's not. You drink—you buy! You buy? You pay now!

I provided you that service completely independent (in most establishments) of the dining room staff. They navigate their way to their table having assumed that the bartender will simply transfer their tab to their new server. You don't go to the mall and walk out of Macy's with a suit that you plan on paying for at Express, so why does anyone think that it's any different at a bar? The *only* exception to this should be if you leave a tip scaled to what the tab would be, and then have it added to your bill at the table. Otherwise, you're stealing.

13

A day in the life

This proved to be one of my favorite parts about observing the bipedal drinking ecosystem. I tailed Jay for an entire workday, from his commute to the watering hole at the beginning of his shift, until the moment he returned home to his dwelling in the wee hours of the morning the following day.

As exhausting as this shift was, it proved to be the glue that stuck all of my individual observations together as one. Also during this time period, I was able to draw more conclusions about what it must be like to tend bar at in one of these environments. As a matter of fact, I just might try my luck behind the stick once this project hits the bookshelves...

***

I'm a big fan of Anthony Bourdain—of his television shows and of his writing. He has a very unique "no holds barred" way of saying stuff. At the beginning of a random sentence or description, he's as poetic as Robert Frost. A few words later, he's dropping a barrage of *F-bombs* like a dirty comedian on stage during a coke binge.

For those of you who may be unfamiliar with this connoisseur of travel, culture, and cuisine, he's the host of the Travel Channel's *No Reservations,* CNN's *Parts Unknown,* and the author of several fantastic culinary books including *Medium Raw* and *Kitchen Confidential.* It was in the latter of the two that he took several pages to narrate a day in the life of a chef; from the moment he opened his crusted-over eyeballs to the shutting of them many, *many* hours later.

Bourdain goes on to describe in great detail the stressors, challenges, excitement, and glory all in a hard day's work from behind the line. I figured that I should do the same— sub bartender for chef, of course. Here's every detail that I could conjure-up from an average Friday night drink slinging session at the Irish pub.

4:30 pm

It's Friday, and I'm on the way into work. My musical choice for the commute is a collection of hymns from the warrior poet Earl Simmons, aka DMX.

DMX? Yeah, I know. It's just that his rambunctious barking and yelling winds me up like the energizer bunny on bath salts. No coffee is needed yet as I blast *Ruff Ryder's Anthem* with my windows down. I aggressively kick open the door to the pub like a DEA agent looking for crackheads, and charge back behind the bar to greet everyone, still grinding my teeth and humming the lyrics to *Where The Hood At.* The natives of the watering hole seem a bit spooked—their eyes are now wide, brows up, and their pint and martini glasses remained suspended touching their lips. I can't help the excitement—I absolutely love this job.

It's busy at the beginning of my shift, and a bit chaotic as the daytime bartender begins to brief me on deliveries, what we've 86'd (what we've run out of), who's had what to drink and how many, the tabs that are open at the moment and those that they're trying to close out, etc. All of this briefing takes place as I walk around the bar shaking babies and kissing hands.

Naturally, I tend to miss a lot of this briefing being that I have the attention span of a goldfish. The daytime bartender will usually hint to his or her guests that their shift is coming to an end, and that they would like to close their tab out. In other words, they want to get paid for their service. It's an awkward discourse, but it's a necessary one. It would be similar to a car salesman in the middle of making a deal allowing another salesperson to swoop-in and take their client halfway through the process. No bueno. Usually, the guest is fine with closing their tab and beginning a new one with the newly arrived crew. But if they're stubborn about it, the night crew will usually collect any gratuity and submit it to be collected by the daytime bartender the next day.

As the transition is underway and almost complete, I am tasked with counting my drawer up to $500. It's imperative that I do this, because if my cash drawer is short at the end of the night, I am responsible for covering that difference. I may not have had anything to do with the drawer being short money, but because I didn't count it out in the first place, I pay the piper.

OK, so now that my cash drawer is calibrated and I've got my bottle popper secured to my right forearm with a tennis sweatband, now what? Usually, the first thing I do is scan the bar supplies to make sure there are no holes or gaps in our stockpile of liquor, beer, mixers, fruit, etc. There are few things more annoying and momentum-shattering than having to cut fruit behind a busy bar as the thirsty undead grab at you to have their glasses filled.

Like most human beings, bartenders are indeed creatures of habit. It is said that a good bartender with a well-prepared bar should be able to serve drinks blindfolded. Our anal, obsessive-compulsive reliance on routine and placement rival that of a Marine drill sergeant. Any deviation of this routine will result in utter chaos, panic, and lots of profanity.

Not too long ago, our brilliant management team, apparently fresh off of reading another restaurant management 101 book, decided it was a good idea to move our glass washing machine from one side of the bar to the other after it has remained there for almost four years. Fucking micro-managers! This change came on a Friday morning, two weeks before our busiest weekend of the year —Saint Patrick's Day weekend.

5:30 pm

With dinner reservations out the wazoo and three people deep at the bar, Greeny, Kat, and I are pacing back and forth like recently decapitated chickens completely out of our element and rhythm. We're normally speedy and efficient behind the bar, but right now we look like amateurs. We're forgetting to pour drinks immediately after taking an order or pulling a service ticket, we're breaking glasses everywhere, and we're failing to remember food orders from our loyal guests. We look lost.

Several times already, due to muscle memory and habit that has been formed from working behind the same bar for years, I removed a warm, half-empty pint glass from the bar and emptied it onto a rack of freshly washed glasses—the spot where the glass washer was no more than twelve hours prior. When you see an experienced bartender out of rhythm, more often than not it's because something is out of place. Either that, or they're high on something.

You don't rearrange a chef's station in the kitchen the morning before a busy dinner shift, nor do you reassemble a soldier's field pack before a nighttime incursion. If you do so, you risk the possibility, or better yet—the *inevitability* of committing major errors.

Everything is now where it should be (aside from the glasswasher) and our flow is beginning to be restored. I make sure that Wild Bill's glass is still at least one-quarter of the way full, and if it isn't, I make haste to the tap and pour him a fresh Yuengling.

He's an extremely patient and polite regular, but that doesn't make me feel like any less of an asshole when I see an empty glass in front of him. I make a scene. *"Alam, Alam,"* I yell in a startled German accent reminiscent of my favorite WWII movies as I bolt to get him a fresh pint. After placing it in front of his chuckling face, I bow and plead for his forgiveness. He laughs and obliges.

The DMX high is starting to wear off, and so it's time to make myself a coffee. I prefer an iced coffee as it will keep me hydrated and better able to fend-off an abrupt crash afterwards. Sometimes, I pour a little Baileys in there as a cream substitute or even a little chocolate syrup if I'm feeling squirrely.

The place is really starting to fill up now that happy hour is in full-swing and the dinner rush is beginning. We make one last effort to stock the bar as efficiently as possible before hunkering in for the long haul.

Kera and Albert just sat down! I give her a kiss on the cheek and she gives me one back, and then big Al and I shake hands, him nearly crushing my bones with his chimp-like strength. They're always good for a fun talk, a few craft beers, and an offer to be an ordained minister at their upcoming wedding. That's why I love them—who the hell would *ever* trust *me* to marry them?!

Lou and Rose just walked in! Lou is sporting his ear-to-ear smile and his silly high n' tight haircut as Rose greets those around her with warm hugs and kisses. Again, we sprint to the taps, pour their drinks, and try to have them on the bar before they sit down. There is not much more of an honor you can give a bar guest than having a cold one ready and waiting for them as they take a seat.

His drink is a pint of Sam Adams lager, or whatever Sam draft that we have at that present time. Rose's drink is a snakebite—half Harp lager and half Magner's cider. We catch up a bit on the events of the week and exchange new photos of our dogs. After they both get done complaining about their jobs, they love to hear about what kind of trouble Greeny, Kat, and I got ourselves into during the week.

They usually arrive on Friday just as happy hour is kicking into full-gear. Rose's eyes widen and she can barely contain her excitement as she orders her beloved fried chicken sandwich with a side salad and a side of ranch dressing. She's been waiting all week to sink her teeth into that beer-battered bird breast. Lou, on the other hand, decides on the buffalo wings—extra crispy, of course. For as mellow and easy-going as this gentle giant is, dark clouds swirl in the sky outside the bar in a violent, fiery cyclone full of lightning, hail, and vultures if his wings don't come out as such. He spends hundreds of dollars per month at the pub, so make the man's wings crispy, got it?

As much as I'd love to sit here and chat some more while making fun of Lou's haircut and their Chihuahuas, I've got other thirsties at the bar in dire need of assistance, and the servers at service bar do not seem amused by my antics. They're giving me the death glare for not paying much attention to their drink tickets.

As I pluck the service tickets from the printer, I become slightly overwhelmed. I have seven or eight orders to work on, ranging from one to eight drinks per ticket. The confusion sets in as I receive an order to pour an aged Irish whiskey—neat, but on the rocks. It's noted that "neat" means "as is"—*no ice…don't fuck with it; just pour it from the bottle into a glass and lemme at it*. "On the rocks" is bar speak for a drink over ice. Notice the contradiction.

A small hiccup like a misspelling or miss-wording in the assembly line of drink tickets at service bar can briefly throw a bartender off of their game. Add in the hostess barging in to hand you a to-go order, and perhaps a friend or family member demanding a hug, a kiss, and a lengthy catch-up, and you've now fallen behind. In the bar biz, we call this being "weeded." You're drowning in a sea of thirsty, demanding, and unimpressed clientele—they're closing in on all fronts. You're a little defenseless bunny in a high state of panic as the boa constrictor coils around you and begins to rob you of oxygen.

As kegs kick, more bottles drip dry, garnishing fruit runs low, and server tickets keep spewing out of the machine, you consider calling for backup. Personally, there are few things that strip my pride away more than having to call for help to dig myself out of a jam behind the bar. Eight tickets quickly turn into thirteen tickets, and now, aside from the keg, liquor, and fruit supply problems, I have several people at service bar that haven't really gotten the hint that it is not an appropriate place to order drinks. I'm rattled.

Once I have the next ten or so cocktails that I need to build memorized in my head, some drunken bum is able to nab my attention and completely annihilate all of my organization and structure. I'm back to square one as the drink tickets are still being vomiting out of the machine. Without making eye contact, I politely inform the thirsty gentleman that I won't be able to serve him for the time being, and that he'd have better luck with one of the other bartenders. He somehow doesn't get me.

Now drunkenly swaying back and forth like a willow tree's branches in a gusty wind, he loudly demands a double Jim Beam and coke. Thankfully, one of the servers realizes that I'm in some serious doo-doo and gets the guy to bugger off. I yell for my barback, Conor. Where is that little shit?! I'm furious with him for not being around to be able to handle our supply problems. No answer. I yell again. Another server then informs me that they saw him charging towards the back of the house cupping his hand in a pile of napkins and bar rags.

Fuck—he cut himself on some glass.

This is when you must become a hybrid of Buddha, Tom Brady, and a Navy SEAL all at once. You need to breathe and become centered and to find your Zen. Once you do, you must develop a clear vision of what needs to be done, what drinks need to go out before others and to whom, and finally, you must have the mental fortitude to not break under the pressure.

Personally, I love being weeded, for that means that you're busy enough to make some money that night. It's an adrenaline rush to have an obstacle at hand to be negotiated in a timely manner in a hectic environment. It's also fun to put on a show for the bar guests that are amused by the pouring of seven draft beers at once or the octopus-like movements that are made when making several different cocktails simultaneously right in front of them. The machine, I notice, hasn't spat-out a ticket in almost a minute. I'm finally catching up.

7 pm

It's time to pick tonight's winner of the $200 gift card happy hour contest. Like mentioned in the *Happy Hour* chapter, every Friday at the pub we give our guests raffle tickets with every food item that they intend to cram down their gizzard. At 7pm, we announce the winning number and the guest with that lucky ticket gets the gift card. Guerrilla marketing.

I turn on the microphone (which is quite loud and can just about rupture anyone's eardrums in the building) and with my best impression of a clunky, strip club disc jockey, I introduce the contest and its stipulations. Then, I switch to more of a Bruce Buffer (UFC announcer) type of character:

"Ladies and gentlemen, after three long hours of continuous gluttony, we have a winner! The lucky native taking home a two-hundred-dollar gift card to this very fine establishment —orrrr staying here til' last call and blowing all of it tonight —is that person holding the ticket with the last three numbers: blah blah blah."

It's gotten to the point now where the regulars have memorized my speech. It's painfully corny, but it works and they like it.

As the slightly embarrassed winner approaches the bar to claim their earnings, the rest of the hoard moans and mumbles under their breath as they try to deal with defeat. Once the disappointment dissipates, it's back to business as usual.

The lineup of regulars tonight is wonderful, and during brief moments of mindfulness and deep thought, it's quite humbling. These guys don't miss a beat. They're here week-in and week-out to have some drinks, eat, and hang out with us. It's easy, during the duration of the evening, to forget that. It's also easy to succumb to the minor gripes and complaints that we all have at the workplace no matter what type of job we have. We bartenders, however, are their weekly sitcom. It's our job to try our best to not give them a boring or half-assed episode.

Lou and Rose are toasting and laughing to the comedy styles of Wild Bill. Mary, head in her hands, is just marveling at him as he entertains the entire half of the bar, the patrons all leaning in to ensure that they don't miss the punchline. An eruption of laughter ensues.

Traci, another O.G., regular, friend, and Wisconsin Badger loyalist, has also stopped in for a quick meal and a drink on her way back from some important international United Nations, Peace Corps, save the world convention thingy. I catch up with her a bit, and as we exchange stories, thoughts, and ideas, one can't help but notice her smile: it's always bright and shining, even after having the worst of days. I have a quick flashback to a night when Danny, Laff, a few other employees, and myself bumped into her at the pub on one of our off nights. It happened to be her birthday, so we all made it a point to march behind the bar, crank-up the microphone, and sing an awfully painful, yet beautiful rendition of happy birthday to her. She's one of our treasures here at the pub.

Fran is heckling my stupid gold tie again. I still can't believe we have to wear these crappy things. Her and Tom are here to camp-out for a few drinks in anticipatory excitement to yell "Freeee Birrdddd" over and over again at the house band tonight.

The Campbell's and I catch up on events of the past week as she drinks a glass of pinot grigio over ice and he enjoys his Smithwicks Irish ale. It's another workweek down for the Mrs, and as a teacher, looking forward to Friday night at the watering hole is what gets her around the final turn.

The Peppers are getting sloppy. After throwing back a few, Bob likes to get mouthy and enjoys heckling us. Sadly for him, he doesn't have the depth to compete with professional shit-talkers such as yours truly. He is, however, a great guy and always adds a fun energy to the room with his goofy and sometimes bizarre dance moves.

The Sicilian is here and gone after a long work week, a stiff drink, a philosophical reference to Seneca or Marcus Aurelius, and a quick handshake goodbye. I fuggin' love that guy.

Just like the Sicilian, there are others who arrive solo for a beer or two, and just a chance to be in a lively social setting before ending the workweek and going home. Stephen, a military man in uniform, is enjoying a brewski and some soccer talk with Greeny. They get along extremely well given the fact that Arsenal is Stephen's team and Manchester United is Greeny's.

Keith, otherwise known as "Coach," has recently parked his backside on one of our barstools as well. This cat is an incredible human being. I guess you could say that he's a more reserved version of Wild Bill. He usually sits at the same barstool at the very end of the bar if possible. He drinks the same beer—Budweiser—every single time he visits, and always leaves more gratuity than he should.

Getting to know him has been an experience that I am grateful for. He came to us from an adjacent watering hole and has made our pub his impromptu home. He has been caring for his ill mother aside from working a construction gig, and behind his big smile and crows feet that sprawl from the corners of his eyes, I can tell that he's hiding his pain deep down in his gut, trying to subdue it with the "king of beers." I take any chance I get to give him an ear to talk into, but damnit—it's busy tonight! Time to move down the line.

Bob and Marg have made a rare Friday appearance too! They are one of my favorite couples that have ever walked through the doors of the pub and are another example of guests turned into great friends. Bob, a 60-something year-old small-business owner and apparent renaissance man with an interest, knowledge, and background in almost everything, sits beside his lovely wife and business partner, Marg.

Bob drinks anything—Guinness, red wine, gin and tonics, and even mojitos. He seems to have an appreciation and fascination for everything. Marg is much more particular in her drink preferences as she can usually be seen sipping on wine or after dinner liquors. Yet, they're usually both willing to allow me to experiment on them with a new cocktail recipe I've been working-up.

The conversation is never lacking with these two. Bob soon takes over the vast percentage of talking as he goes on about old Navy stories, diving trips, and his motorcycle-racing son whom he absolutely adores. After griping to us about their annoyances in the workplace, we get into a little politics, philosophy, environmental talk, or whatever sparks their interest at that moment. But again, it's busy, so down the line I go.

Kelly, Kelly, Rachel, and Lea have stopped in to give me their love in exchange for a few shots before heading to the beach for the weekend. For as cute and friendly as these ladies are, they can turn into ethanol-guzzling zombies at the drop of a dime. Some of my best memories from bartending at the pub were born from their random Monday or Tuesday night drunken tomfoolery. I, for one, could never keep up with them when I'd occasionally abandon my post to accompany them for the night. Absolute savages, they are, and I love them to death for it.

They do a few rounds of rapid-fire shots of whatever I give them, give me the biggest hugs and softest kisses that make my head spin (and other adjacent bar guests look at me as if I'm some kind of working pimp), and take-off out of my life until the next time I see them.

Courtney, Amanda, Josh, Devin, Zack, Erin, and the rest of their wild band of savages just rolled-in. In typical "them" fashion, they're already white-girl-wasted. They look like they've been through the meat grinder and are begging for me to help them hydrate. One of them is even missing a shoe somehow. It would be unethical to turn-away such desperate creatures, and so I provide medical care for them in the form of whiskey shots. Why not? It's Friday.

Today, Courtney seems disinterested in trying to seduce the microphone away from me so that she can try out her new stand-up comedy material. On other occasions, I was made weak by her smile and cute Castellana accent, and ended up handing it over to her. Her jokes are actually quite hilarious, but what has always proved to be even funnier, is how she reacts to her friends heckling her and demanding that she shut up. Professional stand-ups could probably learn a thing or two from how she handles hostile crowd members.

Joey and Matty, two high-ranking Air Force reservists, have just arrived as well and are seated next to Matty's girlfriend, Aimie. Both of the gents are drinking Jameson on the rocks —a lot of it. Aim, on the other hand, is on her way to creating a worldwide shortage of Patron. They suck them down like fish, so it's important to keep an eye on their glasses. Matty and Joe have been all over the world together and remain best of friends to each other and to us to this day. Think the starring cast of *Super Troopers*—then you'll have a good idea of how funny and goofy these two are.

Katie, Brian, and Swallace—who just got done with his day shift—are doing shots. They're doing *lots* of shots. But after the last round, they wanted to close out their tab because they're headed to black-out somewhere else. As I collect their credit card slip, I see that it's covered with extremely inappropriate images, such as hairy, STD-ridden penises, ejaculating penises, and well, penises of all kinds. On the designated line for gratuity, they have made it clear that it be "just the tip." Nice, guys. Nice. I'm sure the accountant who looks at these things will appreciate your taste in surrealism and puns.

I've spotted Anthony and Tara at the end of the bar so I make my way down there to see them. Just like Mr. and Mrs. Wild Bill, these two lovebirds had their wedding festivities at the pub also. They had requested for me to be their private bartender, and I accepted with a smile from ear-to-ear. It was one of the few times I've been absolutely hammered-drunk behind the bar. If I was a dog and I had a tail, it would always be wagging when I see them walk into the bar.

The real party animals in the room right now though, however, are Tony, Gabe, Eamonn, Peggy, and the rest of their crew. You see, they're *Irish*. That should be enough explanation as is. But, I'll elaborate in that they drink like fish, know every Irish rebel song by heart, and actually have

Irish accents. When you hear people in an Irish pub speak with Irish accents, you know that the place is legit.

With this group, I have to be extra vigilant as their pint glasses seem to evaporate of beer shortly after being filled. These guys come to party, and rarely a night passes with them not bouncing from chair to chair amongst their friends, drunkenly embracing each other, and eventually huddling together in a circle, raising their glasses, and singing IRA songs. Oh! And here we go! They're up and swaying back and forth right now, belting the notes to "Fields of Athenry!" They could certainly use some singing lessons, however.

Glen—a royal pain in the ass with a lingering charm to him— is getting ready to leave. He's been here since before I arrived. He usually gets a ride to the pub after work and comes to pester the daytime bartender as he drinks a pint of Coors Light and a shot of Goldschlager. He's one of the most chatty people I've ever met, and loves, loves, *loves* to float around the room and socialize. The problem with that is, he can be pretty creepy about it at times.

I mean, we all know that he's harmless, but the other natives at the watering hole really don't. I've seen him sit on a couch alongside a family he didn't know at our upstairs bar during a college football game. He's been scolded for changing seats too many times and making a spot for himself at someone else's table—usually occupied by women. As he goes on and on about how wealthy he is (he's not), they look at us and others around the room with rolling eyes and a *please get this guy away from us* expression of desperation. I've even caught him hitting on my sister at the bar, him not knowing that I am her big, short-to-anger, extremely protective brother.

Yet, in all of his annoyance, he's a good guy who somehow makes us laugh after we've expelled all of our angst and frustration towards him. Think Steve Urkel. Sometimes, we want to clobber him when he acts up, but he's always quick to apologize. And when he does, he's a professional at giving the sad puppy eyes, eventually making *us* feel bad for yelling at *him*.

Meg has had enough of Glen's shit, however, and she lets him know it. She's not to be messed with, for sure. She's just arrived—a bit earlier than usual, mind you—and I can tell that Glen is about to get it from her if he doesn't shut his yap. At least that's what I thought at first. Five minutes pass by and now they're laughing together and discussing scenes from the movie *Jaws*. I don't get people, sometimes.

9pm

The dinner rush has come and gone, and it's time to transition to the late-night crowd. Really, there's not much of a change aside from the music and the age of the patrons. As time ticks away, the music gets louder and the drinkers get younger. Also, I finally have time to get out from behind the bar and take a piss. Sadly though, I've been sweating profusely and haven't had much to drink, and so barely anything comes out beyond a few quick streams and drops.

And on the topic of peeing, I find it awkward to stand next to some dude at the urinal, bullshitting about the game on the big screen, him knowing very well that I'll be touching his plate of food and the lime that goes on his jack and coke not

233

long after I have my hands wrapped around my wang. For this, I always try to duck into the handicapped stall that has a locked door. Either that, or I'll just bail through the back exit and draw liquid graffiti on the outside wall.

Anyway, I'm starving now, so I sneak into the kitchen like a neighborhood stray dog looking for scraps of food that the servers have ordered to eat during their breaks. I'm hoping that their meals have been left unattended for a moment so that I can indulge myself. A strip of bacon? *YES!* Cold and soggy fries? *BLISS!* A slice of cheesecake that is waiting to be tossed because it was sliced improperly by the expediter? *GIMME THAT SHIT!*

I beat my chest like a silverback gorilla and bark at them like a Rottweiler, viciously and primitively ordering the servers and food runner to "back away from the cake!" I tell them that no one will be hurt if my demands are met. I eventually win on the grounds of being more desperate for food than the rest, and I cram that stale piece of dessert down my throat and chomp at it, my head jolting from side to side, eyes rolling into the back of my head as I bite down like a thrashing shark tearing apart a tuna.

On the way back to my post, I spot Conor, our barback, carrying two buckets of ice towards the bar, his hand completely bandaged up. What a warrior. Well, he's as about as warrior-esque as a 20-year old, long-haired skateboarding hippie can be. He's been an integral part of our wacky and fucked-up family of bartenders and joke tellers here at the pub.

Conor is pretty quiet during the course of the night— especially when it's busy. On top of him hustling his ass off for random ingredients, ice, and to change kegs, the only time you really notice him is when you see one of the bartenders walking around with a piece of paper taped to their back declaring things like "Call me names for free drinks," "Tonight is my *cumming* out party," and "I'm craving little boy meat."

His primary target is always Kat, who is currently our only female bartender. He likes to make fun of the fact that she used to work at Home Depot by advertising via *post-it* that "I (Kat) worked at Home Depot," and "I'm not funny."

She typically discovers it once she's been insulted enough, and then charges at Conor to regain her honor. The two wrestle and claw at each other, the tussle usually ending with Kat as the winner. I mean, she is pretty strong given that she used to unload trucks and pile pallets of wood at Home Depot in her denim overalls and bright orange hat. (Ow! She just punched me as she's sitting here helping me edit this.)

It's time to get back to work as a bachelorette party just arrived. Now, I'm not trying to downplay or discredit my own place of work, but *this* bar? For a *bachelorette party*? *Really*? Eh, whatever. I'll take the influx of little black dresses and chicks who will probably be feeling pretty lonely and vulnerable by the end of the night after celebrating the upcoming marriage of one of their best friends.

They start ordering drinks and shots just as the band starts ramping up. It's a free-for-all as they are all ordering cocktails for each other but no one seems to want to hand me their cash or credit card. Aside from the constant screeching of the words "freeeee birrrddd" from the mouth of Fran, the belting of Lenny's voice—our house entertainment for the night—interferes with me hearing one of the girls' drink request. Naturally, I signal for her to lean over the bar more and whoops—out pop the titties! Hey, don't judge me. It's a perk of the job.

Two younger, very polite enlisted guys—both Army—have been sitting at the bar since the culmination of happy hour. I always like to make small talk with out-of-town military guests as I know very well the feeling of being stationed somewhere away from home without the comfort of friends or family. I usually make small talk about where they're from, how long they'll be stationed here, past duty stations, and so on.

I could tell that both of them were feeling like fish out of water in this small town, so I cozied-up to a few of the lassies from the bachelorette party and introduced the guys to everyone as my good friends. Psychologically, I feel as if there's a small advantage to being buddies with the host of the party, which in the bar environment, is usually the bartender. Knowing the bartender somehow offers a cloud of credibility and a tangible importance or social status to a guest (unless you're the guy passed out on the bar after fifteen buds and moan my name as you say goodbye and wobble to the toilet). Being good chums with the bartender suggests that they have a good rapport with the one in power, and I think other people subconsciously register it.

It's the same reason why, on a busy night, I'll be greeted by big, hearty hugs and handshakes by people I really don't know that well. I don't think it's even so much as to try to get a drink on the house tab as much as it is to establish an alpha status in the room. They want everyone—their friends, their date, and total strangers to know that they're pals with the bartender—the proverbial host of the gathering.

These two guys didn't ask me to hook them up. I just feel like, even at the smallest level, it might turn out to be a story for them to tell to their buddies back on base. To be honest, I had to learn their names again to make sure that I didn't compromise the mission. They begin to interact almost instantaneously.

As I pour them all shots on the house (a few drops of cheap vodka mixed with a variety of juices), the girls toast the guys and the guys toast them back. We may have something here, folks! The tunes are bumping tonight. Thank God, because our management has had the tendency to book some awful and stoic acts as of late. Not tonight, though. Tonight, my good friend Lenny Fattori is whaling away as a solo act blasting sum dem sweet, sweet reggae tunes, boi!

10:00 pm

Wild Bill, Mary, Lou, Rose, and most of our other collection of beautiful regulars are now closing out their tabs and calling it quits for the evening, realizing that this late-night scene is no country for old men. As Lenny starts playing *Welcome to Jamrock*, I help escort them through the crowd of drunken, humping young folk and safely to the exits where I give them all hugs, kisses, and of course, my thanks. It's stupid how much money they leave us when they visit. But no argument or rationale can convince them of doing otherwise. We make sure to let them know every single time that we care about them deeply.

As I make my way back behind the bar, I see the girls all lined-up and looking thirsty. "What can I do for you ladies?"

"Blow jobs!"

"Well OK then," I say as I smile back. "While I'm making them, ya'll go ahead and tie your hair back. It's about to get messy." I still marvel at what I can get away with saying at my place of work.

A blow job shot is a favorite of the ladies' nights out. They're done in a variety of ways, but I like to mix Irish liquor with Jameson in a shot glass, top it off with whipped cream, then place it atop an upside-down pint glass. The finishing touch is added, which includes adding a sloppy trail of cream down the side of the overturned glass.

There are two rules: hands must be placed and remain behind the shot-taker's back during the consumption of the shot, and you must clean the glass of any and all cream using the tongue and lips. The girls are super excited to take the shots, and needless to say, I'm not upset about my role as referee. Best seats in the house.

As the Army guys watch in awe like virgin math team competitors receiving a strip tease from Jessica Alba, I announce the rules of the shots over the microphone. Now the whole bar is tuned-in to watch ten or so hot chicks in their 20s deep-throat their shots and lick the stems clean of any remaining white goop.

I shout "go!" and they're off like owls licking away at tootsie pops on ecstasy. Boobs flop everywhere. Whipped cream paints their mouths and faces and drips into their cleavage, so they've decided to perform cleanup duties for each other by licking each other dry.

Making out with each other seemed inevitable, and now they're going at it, some uncomfortable, but most loving every minute in their sloppy, sexual spotlight. They've become the life of the room, even more than Lenny who's playing a sick version of *Bullet and a Target* by Citizen Cope.

Midnight

Everyone is getting trashed. What does a bartender do in this situation when it's only midnight and the entire room is already flirting with being cut-off? Pour water for everyone? Try to get everyone to eat late-night pub food? Nay to both. We get the girls on the bar for body shots, of course.

As one girl who still has the whipped cream around the outer part of her lips jumped at the opportunity to let a friend take a body shot off of her, I prepare the shot of tequila. She climbs seductively—and with a surprising amount of coordination—onto the bar surface. The soldiers' jaws plummet to the floor. Out come their smartphones for documentation purposes.

She's wearing very, very tight white denim shorts with a yellow thong poking out of her waist, which is as curvy as Lombard Street in San Francisco. She unbuttons what little amount of clothing remains on her body and snatches the salt out of my hand. As I begin to think about what her father might do to me if he saw this, I drizzle our lowest-grade, cheapest tequila onto her well-sculpted, tanned mid-section and gently place a lime between her lips.

Lenny is taking a break from playing during all of this, so I access the wealth of videos from Youtube and queue-up *Shots* by Lil' John. The music is blaring, the lights are low, and the dancing continues as her friend dramatically climbs on top of this lassie covered in a mess of salt, tequila, and whipped cream. She pulls her shorts down even lower, and with one slow swoop of her tongue, she leaves a trail of saliva on her friend's lower abdomen. Yowza!

12:15 am

As the minutes tick off of the clock, the late-night nocturnals begin to appear. Usually consisting of a blend of local servers, bartenders, cooks, and truck drivers, these creatures of the night are either just finished with their shift and are craving a frothy brew and some time to come down a bit, or getting ready to start their work shift and need a drink or two to take the edge off of reporting to duty. Big Chuck is one of my favorites out of the late arrivals. He works for Six Flags Great Adventure and always has funny stories of dumb tourists doing stupid things while he's at work.

Brian has just arrived at about the same time as Steve—both limousine drivers by trade. Steve is the only guest in the history of the pub to have his own customized glass—a 100,000-ounce goblet from which to slurp beer (my estimation may be a few placeholders off, but who's counting anyway?). They both look strung-out from carting impolite and impatient cliente around the tri-state area all day and night. After both of them exhale deeply expressing their *holy shit it feels good to be here* sentiment, I shake their hands, place a coaster in front of them, and ask "What are ya' havin'?"

They respond simultaneously—*"Anything!"* You can always tell when they've had a rough night, as they will usually sit at the far end of the bar and pay zero attention to the shenanigans happening around them. They just stare into their glasses talking to each other about how much they hate people, completely ignoring the two hot, half-naked 22-year-old girls making out only a few feet away.

12:45 am

Well, I figured that this night wouldn't be complete without some minor fisticuffs. Apparently, a guy started flirting with one of the girls from the party. Unfortunately for him, he was caught by his girlfriend, who then made a beeline for one of the seductive dancing queens, grabbed her by the hair, and basically tried to scalp her. Needless to say, some of the girls in the party jumped-in to protect their make-out pal and began clawing at the jealous girlfriend. This resulted in her boyfriend jumping-in to protect his girl, which then lead to one of the Army guys intervening with him.

Honestly, I was enjoying it. I mean, this is what I'm talking about! If there was a way to silence all of the speaking and music and replace it with the screams of different monkeys or chimps, it would have looked like a shit-fight at the Philadelphia zoo. We're not very far removed, people.

The damage was minor as no hard punches were thrown, nothing was broken, and the guys barely did anything—I'm sure they were worried about being *that guy* who ended up hitting a girl.

All of the perverts in the room, including myself, were actually somewhat pleased with the show, given that lots of clothing had been forcefully removed from several of the girls. The bouncer got everything under control in less than a minute. Peace was restored to the watering hole. (Note: I spotted the jealous girl's boyfriend with the same girl from the party that he was flirting with, together at the bar not long after the incident. Ouch.)

1:30 am

Well, it's finally last call and I realize that the night has passed very quickly. It seems like I was just announcing the presence of Wild Bill entering the bar, but in all reality, nine-or-so hours have slipped away to the abyss. Because it was such a fun night, we've barely done any cleaning.

Normally, in order to save us some time at the end of the night, we clean as we go, methodically stowing away any excess fruit, washing bar utensils, and wiping down bottles. On this night, however, the bar is a mess, and there's whipped cream everywhere.

I turn into public enemy number one when I announce that it's last call. Everyone groans and hisses—I think someone even just threw a head of lettuce and a rotten tomato at me. But nonetheless, I shock them with the ugly lights.

My fellow bartenders and I are exhausted, hungry, and drenched in sweat and spilled booze. But our tip jars appear full to their brims. As if that doesn't make me happy enough, I just saw one of the Army dudes making out with one of the girls from the bachelorette party, and his friend walking out with one of her friends. Ohh men in uniform—so dreamy...

I thank each and every one of the girls from the party for making it a fun, fruitful, and very memorable night, and when I do, they demand to take a picture with their bartenders—the male ones, at least. When Greeny and I walk around and out from behind the bar to oblige them, we're clutched, grabbed, and poked in every which way. Strangely, I don't mind the violation.

As we begin to stack phone numbers in alphabetical order, I notice the bride-to-be at the other end of the bar crying into her hands. *Oh jeeze. Here we go.*

"What's the matter darling?"

"Nuh..nuh…nothingggg," she sobs.

"She's fine, she just…ya know," one of her friends interrupts. Her attempt to silence what was coming proved to be futile.

"We…we don't have sex anymoreeee! I'm twenty-four, and we don't fuck each othererererrrrr!" I can't help but think of that night when Deloris took her sexual dry-streak out on me.

Instantaneously, I see two guys who are paying their tabs look up—their heads tilted and ears pointed like wolves who've just heard a whimpering, injured baby deer alone and moaning in the forest. I could see and hear the saliva building-up in their mouths as they licked their chops.

"Hey girls, so what hotel are you all staying at?"

Bottom-feeding scavengers.

2:10 am

We barely get everyone out of the room before 2am, but when we do, there's a collective sigh amongst all of us. It's over. Another night of slinging drinks and mayhem down.

Now it it's time to get to cleaning. The shit talking starts instantly.

"Did you see the tits on the one brunette with the lip ring?"

"I wanted to bitch slap that guy in the suit from earlier and use his tears as lube to fuck his girlfriend with."

"Dude, who farted?"

"That dumb cunt who told me that her rum and coke tasted fruity was chewing gum the whole time she was drinking it!"

"Those army guys better wrap up their johnsons tonight."

"Yeah, we better sterilize this bar top, I don't want any herpes crawling onto someone's plate of fish and chips."

"That guy grabbed my hand when he first sat down and tried to kiss it! I was like, *NO*, sir! *NO*! Guys are fucking gross."

"This gunk in the drain looks like Deloris' vagina!"

And it goes on and on as we remove the bar mats, cover all of the bottles to prevent the invasion of fruit flies, carry out empty kegs, wipe all sticky surfaces down with sanitizer, take out the garbage, stock beer, and enter our credit card tips into the computer. The bouncer and barback help out with stacking chairs, which is something that no one wants to be doing at this time of the night/morning.

In the past, our late-night cleaning soundtrack has been strange enough, with mopping music ranging from Sinatra, to Native American flutes, to heavy metal, to the Joe Rogan podcast. Lately it's been Miles Davis. In addition to late night tunes, we enjoy the comedy styles of Conor, and our bouncer, the radical Russian—Pete. Pete, an enormous, no-nonsense, *very* conservative financial studies fanatic and competitive bodybuilder grabs the microphone and performs his best WWE impression of what he imagines his own character would be like.

He challenges the masses to come for his belt in a deep and scratchy voice. Then Conor grabs the microphone and starts ranting, as per the episode of *South Park* in which the aliens begin to take everyone's *jerbs.*

"Pete, if yew don't start doin' yer jerb, then they gonna come n' *take* yer jerb!"

The two very unlikely friends joust back and forth in a wrestling match of wit, insult, ball-busting, and stereotype abuse. We roll around laughing in a delirious state until we realize just how late it's getting, and that we eventually need to go home at some point. Back to work, idiots.

As we finally sit at the round table (we like to call it the round table even though it's a rectangle), we pig-out on scraps from the kitchen and whatever the cooks didn't secure or hide well-enough. We continue talking shit about guests and complain about our job until we are hoarse. It's always nice to sit around with everyone, put our feet up, and discuss—in great detail—cocktails, politics, cleavage, religion, sports, quantum physics, and everything in between.

We split-up the tips, stash cash in the safe to be deposited in the bank, stack any un-stacked chairs, and do one last walk-through behind the bar and through the restaurant. In case anyone from the IRS is reading, when we clock-out for the night, we *always* declare *all* of our tips, no matter what.

3:55 am

At this time, we begin to kill the lights. It's fascinating to see a space that was so chaotic only hours ago transform into complete tranquility. Nothing much can be heard now aside from our footsteps on the rustic, hardwood floors and the periodic ice avalanches falling inside of the ice machine.

The creatures of the watering hole have dispersed for the night, some to slumber and others to move onto other nocturnal activities such as heading to the casino, or ripping the bong at an after party. Regardless, peace and quiet has been restored to the watering hole.

As we leave, we always hi-five. I don't know if many other people do this at other kinds of jobs, but I love it. It's like we're a sports team congratulating each other on yet another victory.

On my drive home my eyes become heavy even though I still feel wired. It's a strange sentiment. It seems like it was forever ago when I was pulling into work like a caged dog who was poked with a stick for weeks, in a state of revved-up happy agitation, grinding my teeth and grunting DMX lyrics. It's a few minutes past 4am now, and I see some folks getting into their cars with briefcases, dressed in business attire as we cross paths at that exact polar opposite moment of our day—the beginning for some and the end for others.

When finally I arrive home, I try not to eat anything because I usually end up getting an upset stomach around 9am the following day. As I collapse onto my bed, I can't help but reflect on my shift. I'm too tired to read but my adrenals still haven't cooled off completely. I grab the TV remote and tune into the strange programming that dwells between the hours of 3am and 6am. After getting sucked into watching that sad Sarah Mclachlan pet commercial over and over again, I settle on a nature documentary about the Serengeti and the interaction amongst all of the different animals at one of the terrain's many drinking holes.

I lay there and ponder something interesting as I drift off to sleep: *Wouldn't it be interesting to document the ecosystem of **my** watering hole...*

After Hours

Believe it or not, this idea originally came to me while I was in a comatose state after a Friday night shift as I sank into my bed while watching a nature documentary about the watering holes of the Serengeti. The cracked-out zoologist's narration, paired with the funny interaction of the animals (along with a substance or two I may or may not have ingested), left me feeling very entertained and extremely giggly. I couldn't help but think to myself that this same guy should do a documentary at the pub.

The light bulb was illuminated and I immediately went to work. I told myself that I was going to write a book, but part of me didn't really believe that I would. Not too many other people believed it either. I recalled memories and thoughts, and conjured new observations of the behavior of those that surrounded me on a busy Friday or Saturday night, and got to scribing. Over two years later, I'm sharing it with everyone who'll give it a look.

For me, bartending has been a blessing more so than a curse. Rarely have I dreaded going into work behind the stick. In fact, I usually can't wait to don my sweatband that anchors my bottle popper to my arm, set-up my bar, and begin hosting friends and strangers alike. Bartending is a fun job, and for the most part, it's always treated me well.

No matter what kind of shitty day or week I was having at the time, I knew that soon enough, I'd be heading into sling drinks. The outside demons that I was battling at the time were 86'd when I walked into the job. I got really good at losing them at the door, for I was now going on stage. I was addicted to the scene, and more importantly, to the people.

And just as any person who has found success would advise, I immersed myself in what I enjoyed doing, and through that, I found a way to document it and all of its strangeness in literature. All of the long nights, good tippers, bad tippers, awkward discussions, nudity, and drunken shenanigans—all of the people—the people were so special to me that writing about them became a way to immortalize them in written word.

My life has changed a lot since I started bartending—mostly for the better. I've moved around, tried new things, worked different jobs, loved, lost, and longed. But the one constant has been the unique feeling of camaraderie that I've experienced after becoming one of the tribesmen—one of the natives at the watering hole.

I am in no way, shape, or form the best bartender you'll come across. I can't recite to you loads of facts and information on different peating techniques of small-batch whiskeys, nor can I debate you on the intricacies of Rioja versus Burgundy wines. And I sure as hell can't flip bottles around without breaking anything. But what I do as well as anyone, in my humble opinion, is observe and appreciate what I do for a living, and of course, the company it holds.

And so, aside from leaving twenty-percent the next time you go to your local watering hole, I ask you to share this book with others. Tell them it's a great book to read whilst sitting on the shitter and taking a mean dump, or tell them that it can teach them the secrets to sculpting a six-pack or even getting laid. Tell them whatever you have to. Because when it all comes down to it, I enjoy telling stories, and I want the world to know about Wild Bill and Mary, Danny, Lou and Rose, Deloris, Traci, Meg, Art, Joey and Matty, Kat, Laff, Kelly, The Sicilian, and the rest.

Without them, I wouldn't have many stories to tell.

About the Author

First and foremost, Jay Reid is a bartender. He's not the best and he's not the worst. He simply loves it more than most.

A native of Trenton, New Jersey, Jay's eyes widened when he stepped behind the bar for the first time, and was instantly struck by the magic that a barroom can evoke. Since then, whether he knew it or not, he has been compiling thoughts for his first book 'The Watering Hole.'

Always an adventurer, a joker, and an enthusiast for the bizarre, Jay, who currently resides in San Diego, seems to have found his calling as a storyteller.

***

To take a deeper look into the works of Jay, or find out where you can have him pour you a proper drink, please visit his website at JayReidWrites.com.

Follow him on Twitter @jayreidwrites

About the Artist

Lin Jones is a freelance artist based out of San Diego, CA. He's been involved in art and music for as long as he can remember, and even points to vivid memories of singing to the flowers around his house while growing up. Art is his self-proclaimed way of exploring the universe. His style is exotic and imaginative, incorporating a wide spectrum of vibrant colors to express his ideas. Lin can occasionally be spotted frequenting watering holes throughout San Diego, and enjoys a delicious, mouth-pinching IPA or a smooth shot of reposado tequila.

***

To view more works of art by Lin, please visit his website at www.linjones.com